From Pain to Purpose

A Journey of Loss, Strength, and Life Lessons

By

SAMI WALKER

Copyright © 2026 by Sami Walker

All rights reserved.

No part of this book may be reproduced or distributed.

In any form without permission from the author.

This book is a work based on real life experiences.

I dedicate this book to my parents,

who gave me life and taught me the meaning of love and sacrifice.

To my two sons,

who have always been a part of my strength and my reason to keep going.

And to my niece,

whose support, kindness, and presence in my life reminded me that even in difficult times, we are never truly alone.

AUTHOR'S NOTE

This book tells the true story of my life and the journey my family and I experienced over many years. The events, struggles, and lessons described here are real.

For personal and safety reasons, I have chosen not to mention the name of the country where I was born. Some members of my family and people connected to my past still live there, and I do not want my story to create any risk or difficulty for them. Because of this, certain locations and details remain general.

What matters most in this book is not the name of a country, but the human journey itself—the search for safety, freedom, dignity, and a better life for one's family.

I share this story honestly, hoping that readers can understand the experiences of people who are forced to leave everything behind and begin again in a new place. If this story can offer even a small lesson, comfort, or understanding to someone else, then writing it has been worthwhile.

CONTENTS

Introduction

Every person has a story.

Some stories are filled with happiness, some are filled with struggle, and most are a mixture of both. Life rarely moves in a straight line. It takes us through moments of joy, moments of pain, and moments where we question everything we thought we understood.

This book is the story of my life.

It is not a story about perfection or success. It is a story about experiences, mistakes, losses, lessons, and the search for meaning. Everything written in these pages comes from real moments that shaped who I became.

Like many people, I experienced love, family, responsibility, and hope. I also experienced loss, separation, loneliness, and the difficult challenge of starting again when life does not go as planned.

There were times when I felt strong and confident, and other times when I felt completely lost. There were moments when life seemed full of possibilities, and moments when it felt like everything I had built was falling apart.

But through all of these experiences, life continued to teach me.

It taught me about the value of family and the pain of losing the people we love. It taught me about

responsibility, forgiveness, and understanding others. It taught me that failure does not define us unless we allow it to stop us from moving forward.

And perhaps most importantly, life taught me that even after pain, it is possible to find purpose again.

This book is not only about what happened in my life. It is also about the lessons that came from those experiences. If my story can help even one person think differently about their own life, then writing these pages will have been worth it.

We are all walking our own paths in life. Some paths are easy, and others are full of obstacles. But every path can teach us something valuable if we are willing to learn.

This is my journey—from pain to purpose.

Chapter 1

Childhood and Early Life

Before I Knew Anything.

No introduction.
No explanation.
Just the truth

I don't remember my childhood clearly, but I remember how it felt.

I was just a kid, maybe five or six years old. I don't remember anything before that. I was born into a big family, and before the war, life was simple and full in a quiet way.

We had land. A farm with date trees, fruit trees, vegetables, cows, chickens, and ducks. We didn't have much, but we had enough. I remember waiting for my father to come home, and I remember feeling safe when he was there.

One day, my father bought me a bicycle. I remember how happy I was, but I don't remember how many times I rode it. Maybe once. Maybe more. What I remember clearly is that one of my older brothers rode it one day, and it broke.

My father took the bicycle to a relative who lived a bit far away to fix it. I waited for it to come back. It never did.

Before the bicycle was fixed, the war started.

After we left, I became quiet.

I don't remember the road. I don't remember carrying anything. I don't remember the noise. I don't even remember my mother's face clearly, not until I grew older and started going to school — maybe not even until the fourth or fifth grade.

It wasn't only my mother. For a long time, faces didn't stay with me. People didn't stay clearly in my memory. Everything felt distant, like life was happening, but not fully touching me.

Still, my mother was the person I loved the most in my life. I didn't always know how to show it, and I didn't always understand it then. Later, when I grew up and got married, everything changed between us. In some ways, it became harder than when I was a child. That part of my life comes later.

What disappeared first was my childhood.

When I started going to school, life began to move again, but I didn't feel like I moved with it.

I remember the first day of first grade in public school. My mother took me there. We walked all the way from our home to the school. It felt long — maybe half an hour — but I was a child, and distance felt different then.

This was during the first year of a war that would last eight years.

I didn't know the road to the school. I don't remember how we arrived there that day. What I remember clearly is that I returned home by myself. From that day on, I always went alone.

I walked to school in winter and summer. In the cold and rain. In heat that sometimes reached fifty degrees Celsius. I didn't question it. I didn't complain. It was just what life required.

By then, we had already moved from our hometown to a small city, about four hours away from where we used to live. Everything was new, but I learned the same thing I had learned before — how to manage on my own.

I was still a child, but something inside me had already grown up.

When I walked to school alone, I didn't feel fear. I didn't feel courage either.

I didn't feel anything at all.

I don't remember carrying books. I don't remember being tired. We didn't have school uniforms then. We wore simple clothes — pants and a shirt, sometimes long sleeves — nothing short. We wore whatever we had, and we didn't think much about it.

In the classroom, I was quiet. I stayed quiet as I grew older, even in high school. I was usually the quietest person in the room. In primary school, we had one teacher for the whole year. I don't know if he noticed me or not. Later, in high school, when each subject had a different teacher, maybe some of them did.

I never felt proud of myself for managing alone. I was just a child. I didn't know anything about life yet, so there was nothing to be proud of. This was simply how things were.

The only time I felt lighter at school was during the breaks. When we played with the other kids between classes, something loosened inside me. For a few minutes, I wasn't quiet or distant. I was just a child again.

Then the bell rang, and I returned to silence.

I don't remember having close friends in primary school. I don't remember names or faces clearly. What I remember is more like a shadow — the feeling that I was there, playing with other kids without fully belonging to anyone. During playtime, I think I was included. We ran together, laughed together, and shared the short freedom between classes. But once school ended, those memories faded.
Outside school, my life was different.

We had neighbors living very close to us, and they had children my age. They were my real friends. We played together after school, during holidays, and whenever we had the chance.

Football was everything to us.

We played until we were tired, until we fell, until our shirts were soaked with sweat. Even when someone got injured, we kept playing. We didn't know it then, but that was how we were learning resilience.

I wasn't the loudest, the fastest, or the best player. I was simply there — part of the rhythm of the game. When the ball rolled through the dust and someone shouted in excitement, everything around me felt lighter.

For a few moments, I wasn't quiet or distant.

I was just a child. Those football days were simple, but they were pure. We didn't know life was complicated yet. We only knew the next pass, the next run, the next laugh. And sometimes I miss those days — not because they were perfect, but because they were free.

Football Was Life

Football filled most of our days after school.

We played until the light disappeared and darkness slowly took over — until we could no longer see the ball. The ball itself was never real. It was plastic. We made it from a few plastic balls because they ripped quickly. We kept the one with the best air inside, and when it tore, we replaced it with another. If we had old balls, we used those first and saved the new one for later.

We played barefoot on muddy ground full of small stones. Our goals were simple — sandals, big stones, or empty cans. When night came and there was no light, when we were thirsty and tired, we still didn't want to go home.

For me, football was everything. It was like food and water. It was life. I never reached anywhere with it. Not because I didn't love it, and not because I didn't know how to play. My parents didn't know much about sports. My father was a farmer — a hard worker, kind and strong — but in his world success came from work, not from play.

When I played football, I did it without him noticing.

He didn't agree with it, and I don't blame him. He simply didn't know another way.

Sometimes I wonder what would have happened if I had been born into a different family — if someone had seen how I played and supported it.

I know I was good. I ran constantly. I defended, I dribbled, and I cared about my teammates, even when there were only two players on each side. I played with boys older than me, and when teams were formed, both sides always wanted me.

I still miss those days — playing in the dirt, in winter and summer — because nothing has made me happier since.

One day, while we were playing, the ball rolled down a small hill next to the field. I went to get it. I climbed using one hand and held the ball with the other.

Suddenly, a broken piece of glass went deep into my wrist. It almost cut my artery. I lost a lot of blood.

We didn't know what to do. We couldn't stop the bleeding. The game ended there. Darkness had already begun to settle, and we all went home.

I didn't tell anyone in my family what happened — especially my father.

Every time we played football and my father found out, we were beaten. Still, we never stopped playing.

Sometimes he wasn't home when we returned. Sometimes he was.

Once, after a game, my younger brother was with me. We reached the front door with the ball in our hands. There was nowhere to hide it, so we threw it onto the roof of the living room, planning to take it back the next day when my father left the house.

That plan lasted only a moment.

It was summer. Our house was built around a big open yard. At night we all sat outside — rugs on the ground, eating

together, talking, then sleeping under the open sky because
there was no air conditioning.

My brothers, sisters, my mother, my father — all of us together.

That was one of the best parts of life, and it never came back
the same way once we grew up.

We knocked on the door. It opened.

At that exact moment, the ball slipped from the roof and
dropped right in front of my father.

That night, we were beaten again.

Home, Hunger, and My Aunt

After school, we were always hungry. We came home with
empty stomachs, but once my mother served the food and we
began eating, we forgot how hungry we had been. Hunger

disappeared quickly then. We didn't think about it. We didn't
complain.

I don't remember being sick or cold very often. We played most of the time. We didn't know what tiredness was.

In the mornings, my mother woke us up. I don't remember exactly what time, but I think it was before seven. I always walked to school. I carried the same school bag throughout primary school. It ripped once or twice, and my mother fixed it.

After school, my younger brother and I played together. Sometimes we fought, but it wasn't real fighting. It was just another way of playing.

Most days, I went outside to play football with the neighbor kids. Our house wasn't loud. Life inside felt quiet.

I wasn't afraid of the war. We grew up inside it. Planes flying overhead, shooting sounds — it became normal.

When the war ended, I was fourteen years old. By then I had already seen many people killed — men, women, and even children — from both sides. I learned early that ordinary people pay the price for decisions made by leaders they never chose.

As a child, I was afraid of adults. That fear slowly faded as I grew older.

But there was one person who never frightened me.

My aunt.

She was very old — maybe in her eighties or nineties. I don't know exactly. I learned later that she had been married once, but when she didn't have children, her husband divorced her. She returned to live with her parents, my grandparents. After they died, she lived with her brothers, moving from one home to another every few months.

She didn't own a house. She didn't have children. She didn't have much at all. Just her clothes and a few extra sets to change.

But she was happy. She was kind to everyone. Respectful. Clean. Polite. She never asked for more than what life gave her. She accepted things quietly, without bitterness. Before she died, she stayed in our home.

At night, I prepared her blanket and pillow. We slept on the floor back then — no beds — like many people did. I loved her deeply, and she loved me too.

One morning we were eating breakfast in the living room. She was still sleeping next to us. Around her were the younger ones — me, my brother, my sisters, and my other brothers — while the house remained quiet. She was still sleeping.

I went to wake her up so she could sit with us and eat breakfast.

She didn't wake up.

I noticed her breathing was very weak, not normal. I told my mother. My father came and looked at her, and he understood immediately. She had a stroke while she was sleeping.

They took her to the hospital. The doctors told my father and the rest of the family that nothing could be done. She was between life and death. She could pass away at any moment — that day, or days later. They brought her back home. She stayed with us for three more days, completely unconscious. My mother and the other women fed her water and cared for her quietly until she left this world. That moment stayed with me.

Even now, when I remember her, I want to see her, hug her, kiss her, and stay with her forever. She was the first person I truly loved, and then she was gone.

She loved me too. Not because I did anything special. I respected her. I cared about her. I didn't like hearing people speak badly about her.

She used to tell my mother that I was the one who cared for her the most. I never understood that then. I thought I was simply doing what felt right.

They buried her in our hometown — the city where the war had happened — not the city where we were living at the time.

After the war ended, we were able to visit her grave and speak to her there. Later in life, I understood something else. We don't need to go to a grave to speak to the people we love. They are everywhere. We can talk to them anytime, anywhere.

Their souls stay with us. And I believe they see us.

Chapter 2

Becoming Before I Was Ready

High School — When Fear Became Normal

When we entered high school, things did not become easier.

They became harder — not only because of studying, but because violence became normal.

Teachers hit us more than in primary school.

Not because we were bad kids, but because we were expected to pass.

If you failed even one subject, punishment was waiting.

I remember one time I didn't pass a subject. I don't even remember which one.

The principal took us to the drinking area. It was winter. Very cold.

He ordered us to put our hands under the freezing water.

Then he told us to raise our hands, palms facing the sky.

He didn't hit us with the flat side of the ruler.

He used the narrow edge — the side that cuts pain into the fingers.

He hit us hard. Again and again.

Cold hands.

Cold weather. Sharp pain.

This was not discipline.

It was tormenting.

We were only in Year 7 or Year 8.

At that time, teachers hitting students was normal.

No one complained. No one questioned it out loud.

Inside myself, I asked quietly:

Why do we get punished for not understanding?

Walking to School

We always walked to school.

Sometimes with neighbors, sometimes with boys who were not really friends — just kids from the same street.

In high school, we stopped using school bags.

Carrying a bag was considered childish.

We held our books in our hands.

If there were many, we wrapped them with a rubber band.

That was our way of saying:

We are in high school now.

The Day My Mind Left Me

One morning, while walking to school, a friend and I got to a small fight — nothing serious.

He pushed me. I fell. I pulled him with me.

He landed on top of me.

When he tried to stand up, I pulled him again.

Our heads collided.

The back of my head hit the asphalt — hard.

After that... nothing.

What happened next is something I later learned has a name: Post-Traumatic Amnesia.

I don't remember the fall.

I don't remember getting up.

I don't remember walking.

Suddenly, I found myself standing in front of the school gate.

I looked at the pens in my hand and asked my friends:

"Whose pens are these?"

They said, "They're yours."

I said, "No, they're not mine."

They thought I was joking.

I kept repeating it.

Then they understood something was wrong.

They took me to the school office.

Someone gave me a cup of water and asked:

"What is your name?"

"I don't know."

"Which class are you in?"

"I don't know."

"Who are your parents?"

"I don't know."

And still... They sent me to class.

I sat through the lessons not knowing who I was, where I was, or what was happening.

When school ended, I went home.

I don't know how.

When I reached the door of our house, everything suddenly came back.

My name.

My family.

My life.

I knocked on the door like nothing had happened.

That night, my head hurt so badly I couldn't eat.

I went to sleep hungry and silent.

I never told anyone.

That memory stayed with me forever.

High School: Years 9–12 — The Path Chosen for Me

When I entered Year 9, we were asked to choose something to learn outside of school — a skill, a trade, something we liked.

We had to find someone to learn from and commit to it during the school year.

For many students, this worked well.

They chose for themselves.

But not for me.

I didn't choose my path.

My relatives — older than me, more experienced, and well-intentioned — chose it for me.

From one perspective, what they did was good.

They were thinking about my future.

They believed I would become successful if I learned that specific trade.

And for that, I still respect them.

But they didn't know — or didn't want to accept — my interests, my likes, my inner direction.

At that age, I didn't really have a choice.

When you grow up in a family where older voices are stronger, you are taught to listen — even when your heart says no.

The trade they chose for me was nursing, working in a hospital.

It was not a bad choice.

In fact, it was a very good profession — if it comes from within.

But it didn't come from me.

What I truly loved was something else.

I wanted to be a car mechanic.

I loved engines, fixing things, and understanding how machines worked.

That never happened.

Because when you are not allowed to choose, interest slowly dies.

For four years — one day a week, every school year — I went to learn something I didn't love.

I showed up. I stayed. I went home. But I didn't learn.

Not because I couldn't — but because I didn't want to.

Other students from the same school learned the same trade and became very good at it.

They had interest.

I didn't.

And without interest, time becomes empty.

That period taught me something I understood much later in life:

You can give someone a good path —

but if it's not their path, they won't walk it far.

A Woman Who Treated Me Like a Son

During those four years in the hospital, I worked alongside several nurses.

Most of them were women, older than me.

I was very quiet — not only by nature, but because I didn't feel I belonged there.

I was present, but my heart wasn't.

I learned some things.

Not everything I was supposed to learn — but not nothing either.

I learned how to give injections, something not everyone can do correctly.

I learned basic first aid.

I assisted with dressing wounds and caring for injured patients.

I never did stitches.

I was shy — deeply shy — especially wearing the nurse's uniform.

I didn't like being seen in it.

Whenever possible, I stayed inside the room, avoided attention, and tried to disappear quietly after doing what I had to do.

But there was one nurse.

She was a very kind woman.

Strong, hardworking, and gentle at the same time.

She treated me like her son.

She encouraged me to learn, to stand confidently, and to not be ashamed.

She pushed me — not harshly, but with care.

At the time, I couldn't fully receive what she was giving.

But now, years later, writing these words, I understand her kindness more clearly than ever.

She is no longer in this life.

But I carry her with respect.

I want this book to hold her name —

not loudly, not dramatically —

but honestly.

Thank you for teaching me.

Thank you for seeing me.

Thank you for treating a quiet boy with patience and dignity.

Miss Kari, I miss you.

I hope your soul is at peace.

And I hope, wherever you are, you can feel these words.

After High School — Between What Was Lost and What Was Required

When high school ended, I didn't feel relieved.

I felt quiet.

Not the quiet that comes after noise,

but the quiet that comes when you don't know

what you're supposed to do next.

For years, my life had a structure decided by others.

School.

A trade I didn't choose.

Rules I didn't question out loud.

And suddenly, that structure was gone.

The war had already ended three years before I finished high school.

But peace did not bring things back.

We didn't return to our hometown.

There was nothing left to return to.

Our house was gone.

The animals were gone.

The land we once lived from had turned into reed beds,

overrun and untouchable, with wild boars roaming freely.

Rebuilding from nothing was impossible.

So my father made another decision —

one more made for all of us.

When I finished high school, we moved back to the same city
we had fled from during the war, but not to our old place. My
father rented a house in a different area of the city. That house
later became our own, when he decided to buy it.

We never went back to our original hometown or land again.

We still own it, but it remains only land — unchanged, unused,
and distant.

Even now, as I write this book, it stays the same.

I was nearly eighteen years old then. I didn't want to continue
studying. Not because I was lazy but because I had never
learned why I was studying in the first place.

I went to school without direction,

without a goal,

without knowing who I wanted to become.

Inside me, there was still that child

who ran barefoot on dirt,

who played football until darkness erased the ball,

who felt alive without knowing why.

But I didn't know how to bring that child

into an adult life.

In my country, when boys turn eighteen, the army is
compulsory.

There is no choice.

There is no alternative.

A few months before my eighteenth birthday, I made a decision that felt practical, even if it didn't feel right. I chose to go to the army and finish the two years of compulsory service instead of wasting time standing still.

There was something else inside me, too — something I rarely said out loud.

I wanted to be free.

Free to talk.

Free to choose.

Free to live without being watched, controlled, or restricted in simple ways.

I used to look at other countries and wonder how people could live with more freedom, with more rights, with less fear of authority. I dreamed of leaving — not because I hated my country, but because I wanted a life where I could breathe. But leaving required money.

And leaving required finishing the army first.

Only then could I apply for a passport.

Only then could I cross a border, even to a neighboring country, and begin again.

At that time, I didn't know that this dream wouldn't happen when I was single.

I didn't know it would come much later after marriage, after children, after life had already shaped me in ways I didn't choose. All I knew was this: I wasn't moving forward. I wasn't moving backward. I was standing between what had been lost and what was required of me next.

Life Inside the Country — Before the Army

We didn't have the freedom to talk openly about the government.

If we talked, we talked quietly — only among people we trusted completely.

Sometimes even neighbors worked with the government, and you wouldn't know.

So you had to be careful:

with drivers, shop owners, strangers, even people who smiled at you.

The government promised many things, but they never delivered. They did whatever they wanted and never cared about people's lives. Our city was the second most important city after the capital.

Before the government came to power, many European families used to visit it for holidays. It was a beautiful place, full of life, friendly people, and pride.

After the war, nothing was rebuilt properly.

In fact, things became worse.

We had the biggest oil refinery in the country — once one of the biggest in the world. Yet when you walked through the city, you saw poverty everywhere:

unemployment, homelessness, theft, unsafe streets, broken
roads.

People were not living the life they deserved.

Fear was always present. Fear of the government.

Fear of the police — even if you had done nothing wrong.

We were treated differently because our mother language was
not the main language of the country. We were looked at
differently, spoken to differently, and rarely respected as equals.

That was one of the main reasons I knew I couldn't live there
forever.

I am a human being — no different from anyone else.

Language, religion, color, nationality — all of these come after
humanity.

When people die, they all return to the same earth. No one is
buried higher than another.

The only thing that truly separates people is how they treat others.

My Inner World at Eighteen

I wanted to leave the country not because I hated it,

but because I couldn't breathe inside it.

We didn't have freedom to speak.

We didn't have freedom to move.

We didn't have freedom to live fully.

Freedom is not just wearing what you like or walking in the street.

Freedom is much deeper than that.

Without freedom, life becomes small and heavy.

I used to see other countries through television and through people who traveled and came back to visit their families. One of my neighbors used to talk about life outside, and every time I listened, I wondered why we couldn't live like that.

I felt stuck. Lost.

Some mornings I woke up hopeful.

By night, I was disappointed again.

No one gave me direction.

One of my brothers told me to go to university, to study and build something for myself. But I refused. Not because education was bad — but because once again, it felt like a path chosen for me.

I had already lived that life. Football was never seen.

My interests were ignored.

My trade was chosen by others.

If someone had asked me then, "Who are you?"

I would have answered with my name.

But the truth is, I didn't know who I was.

That confusion stayed with me for years — even after marriage.

Lack of education, no mentor, no guidance — I paid for all of it heavily.

Most of what I know today came from mistakes.

Mine — and others. I had many dreams.

Some I spoke about quietly. Most I never said out loud. I didn't reach nearly all of them. And that truth stayed with me — not as anger,but as something I learned to carry and move forward with.

Chapter 3

The Army

Discipline, Obedience, and Survival

I joined the army before I turned eighteen.

Not because I wanted to be a soldier,

but because there was no other door open at that time.

In my country, the army was compulsory for boys.

It didn't matter who you were, what you dreamed of, or what you believed.

You went — or you paid a price you couldn't afford.

The first step was reporting to one of the government organizations in our city at a specific time. From there, they would decide where to send us. No information. No explanations.

That morning, I packed a small bag with spare clothes, not knowing where I was going or how long it would take before I could come home again. My mother prepared dates mixed with nuts and sesame seeds for me to take. That was it. Nothing else.

When I arrived, I saw many other boys — some my age, some a little older. Some came with their parents or relatives. Others, like me, came alone.

By midday, everything was finished. Around 150 of us were divided into three full buses. Without warning, they took us to the capital city — an eighteen-hour drive from home.

When we arrived, they gave us army clothes. I don't remember staying the night there. Soon after, they told us we had one week to report to another location to officially begin the two-year service.

This time, we had to travel back home on our own.

A few of us who had become friends during the long bus ride stayed together. We went to the bus terminal, booked tickets, and made our way back home — a journey that took more than twenty-four hours.

At home, there was no time to rest. We had to prepare quickly: adjust the uniforms, buy the few required items, and get ready to leave again. Before the week ended, we left two days early to make sure we arrived on time.

Seven of us from the same city decided to travel together.

That was the beginning of basic training — also known as boot camp or recruit training.

It lasted four months, with no holidays.

The training was hard — physically and mentally.

Every day was a repetition: wake up on time, sleep on time, eat on time. We lined up for food, one by one. It wasn't like home food. But you ate whatever you were given.

They pushed us again and again, even when we were exhausted.

Through it, we learned discipline, cleanliness, responsibility, endurance, and how to live in harsh conditions.

Some people couldn't survive it.

One of the seven friends who came with us ran away from the training camp and never returned. He struggled with drugs, and the pressure was too much for him. He wasn't the only one. Others from different cities escaped at night while everyone slept. The camps were large, and somehow, they found a way out.

During those four months, we were given only a few hours of permission to go into the city to buy necessities. Then it was straight back to the camp.

After the four months ended, we were sent home briefly. I don't remember if the leave was one week or two, but it was short. Seeing family again reminded us of everything we were missing: freedom, home food, warmth, normal life.

Soon after, we were sent to another city for three more months of training.

This time, not everyone went to the same place. From our original group, only six of us remained together. The new location was much colder. We came from a hot city, and winter there was harsh.

The journey itself took nearly twenty hours, with two buses and a long transfer in between. The training there was even harder than before.

At the end of those three months, they took us to the desert for one week to learn survival skills. We slept in tents, in cold weather and rain. It was difficult — but we completed it.

During this time, I became especially close to one of my friends who suffered from night blindness (nyctalopia). He was kind, quiet, and simple — like me.

At night, he couldn't see anything. Whenever he needed to go to the toilet, I held his hand and guided him there, then brought him back to his place. In the first training camp, the toilets were closer than the second one.

In the second, they were far away, and walking in the dark was dangerous for him.

To be honest, he should never have been taken into the army.

But he completed the full two years — and even more, because they punished him with extra service for small, meaningless reasons.

He suffered a lot. I saw it.

And there was only so much I could do.

The army taught us how to stay hungry.

How to stay awake while others slept.

How to guard.

How to endure hardship.

But more than that, it taught us the value of home, family, food, freedom — and silence.

And this was only the beginning.

From Recruit to Trainer

After seven months of continuous training, none of us knew what would come next.

We were still bound to complete two full years of compulsory military service, but where we would go — and what we would become — remained unclear.

At the end of the third training phase, we were separated once again. Small groups were formed and sent to different locations, each with a different responsibility. Because we had completed high school, we were given more responsibility than most. Some of us would become trainers, teaching new recruits what we ourselves had just learned. Others were assigned to administrative work — counting soldiers, managing leave requests, recording absences, and handling paperwork. Those with specific skills were sent to hospitals or technical units.

Even then, nothing was explained clearly.

We didn't know what role we would actually be given until we arrived.

After a short break — no more than one or two weeks we returned home. We visited our families, prepared ourselves mentally and physically, and waited. There was no certainty, only orders.

When I arrived at the new location, I was still with a few close friends — including my friend who suffered from night blindness, one friend from my city, and two others we had grown close to during training. But this place was enormous. Once we reported for duty, we were immediately separated and assigned to different sections. From that point on, seeing each other became rare — sometimes once a week, sometimes after weeks had passed. I was assigned as a trainer. The truth is, I didn't feel ready. I had learned how to endure training, not how to command others.

My friend with night blindness was also assigned as a trainer. From that moment, I could no longer help him at night as I used to. We were responsible for different sections, each bound by our own duties. It hurt me to know he was struggling alone, but in the army, compassion often has no place.

I was sent to a unit of more than two hundred soldiers —
maybe closer to three hundred. They were already at the end of
their four-month training period, not beginners. Around me
were other trainers with far more experience than I had. They
had joined the army before me and knew exactly how to control
soldiers, how to make orders obeyed without question.

I didn't.

The first weeks were difficult.

Some soldiers listened to me. Others didn't.

I struggled to assert authority, and I paid for that internally. But
after about two weeks, that group was transferred to other
locations, and I was given another chance — this time with new
recruits.

Slowly, I learned.

Training soldiers is not about shouting.

It is about presence.

Controlling two to three hundred soldiers every day is not easy. You are responsible for everything: attendance, discipline, cleanliness, food schedules, sleep routines, conflicts, sickness, reports. Every night, reports had to be written and submitted by morning to senior officers — officers for whom the army was not temporary, but a lifetime career.

We trainers were still soldiers ourselves.

The only difference was education.

Some of the men we trained couldn't read or write their own names. And yet we were responsible for shaping them.

By the time a new group of more than two hundred recruits arrived, I was ready. From the very first day, I showed them who I was. Not through cruelty — but through firmness. By the first night, when they saw me approaching, I could hear them whisper to each other:

"Be silent — he's coming."

In the army, kindness without authority is a weakness.

And weakness is punished — by soldiers and officers alike.

I became harder because I had to. Not because I wanted to.

We trained them in everything — from discipline to how to lace their boots properly. We guarded them day and night, sometimes staying awake for twenty-four hours straight. We slept in separate quarters, ate the same food, and carried the same exhaustion.

But something changed in me.

At night, when it was my duty to gather them before sleep, I spoke to them — not as a trainer, but as a human being. I spoke about family. About mothers. About freedom. About the simple things they would miss one day — choosing when to sleep, when to eat, when to leave the house.

I wasn't speaking to them. I was speaking to myself.

And they felt it.

Many of them respected me not because I was strict, but because I was fair. By the end of their training, some gave me their home addresses and asked me to visit them one day. Later in life, I did visit a few of them.

The army taught me discipline, responsibility, and endurance.

But it also taught me how easily humanity can disappear under authority.

I completed my two years of service in that place — with a few extra days added for something as small as letting my hair grow slightly longer than allowed. By the final months, time stopped moving. Each day felt like a year. The last days felt endless.

And then, one day, it ended.

I received my military ID.

I walked out. I went home. I believed I was free. But standing outside the system, a new question followed me: What now?

Chapter 4

Leaving Home

After the Army: Learning to Move Again

When I came back home after finishing the army, I thought freedom would feel complete.

Instead, it felt unfamiliar — like learning how to walk again after standing still for too long.

One of the first things I wanted was a driving license. Driving meant movement. Choice. Escape.

While I was still in the army, I had driven an army Jeep once or twice. A close friend of mine was the driver for a surgeon, and when he let me drive, something inside me woke up. From that moment, I started dreaming about driving — about roads, distance, and motion. But dreams needed money, and I had none.

I worked wherever I could: construction, small labor jobs, buying and selling cigarettes, anything that came my way. Nothing was stable. One month of work could be followed by months of nothing. Still, my focus stayed on driving. I saved slowly, lesson by lesson, until I could afford a few hours with an instructor. I failed the driving test more than once — I wasn't ready, and I knew it — but in the end, I passed.

I had a license. But I had no car. Around that time, home became heavy.

My father had worked his entire life, and he couldn't accept seeing his sons sitting at home without work. Especially me. When I was unemployed, his voice became louder, sharper. I understand him now — but back then, it hurt deeply. I started avoiding him.

I wouldn't wake up in the morning until he left the house. When he came back, I would leave — stand in the street, sit with friends, waste hours just to avoid hearing disappointment in his voice. Those days felt dark. I thought they were the worst days of my life. Later, I learned they were not — but at the time, they felt unbearable.

The only place that felt soft was my mother.

I was very close to her. She was kind, gentle, and always worried about everyone except herself. She suffered from heart problems, cataracts in her eyes, and goiter in her throat. Whenever she needed a doctor or a hospital visit, I was the one who took her. I did it from my heart — because loving her was easy.

After I got my license, I began working as a driver by renting other people's cars and earning a percentage. It wasn't good money, but it was enough to survive. Most importantly, it gave me mobility. I could take my mother to the hospital without begging anyone. That alone made the struggle worth it.

For a period, I also ran a small kiosk near our house, selling cigarettes, chips, and soft drinks — sometimes alone, sometimes with one of my brothers. The kiosk was on the main road that divided the city in two.

And that road changed my life. On the opposite side lived a girl. She belonged to the part of the city connected to the oil refinery — a world that felt separate from ours. I didn't know her name at first. I only knew the way my heart reacted when she walked out of her house. Eye contact was all we had — and somehow, it was enough. I waited for those moments.

I waited for her to leave for school, and later to come back. Just a few seconds each time. My heart beat louder than traffic. I felt — without words — that she felt the same. It was my first love.

We didn't talk. We didn't walk together. She was still in high school, and I was already twenty, just out of the army. Later, through my younger sister — who studied with her — I learned her name. My sister became the bridge between us. Messages passed quietly. Feelings confirmed gently.

One day, after everything was carefully arranged, I picked her up with the car I was working with at the time. It was the first time we spoke properly. I dropped her back near her house, careful not to be seen. She was afraid her father would never accept me — because of ethnicity, language, and the invisible lines that divided our city long before we ever noticed them.

At the same time, I was driving taxis, selling cigarettes, working wherever I could — and still thinking about leaving the country. The desire to leave never went quiet. It waited patiently in the background of everything. Love had entered my life. Responsibility was already there.

Freedom still felt unfinished.

And I was standing at the beginning of a road, without knowing where it would take me.

Between Love, Duty, and Leaving

While I was slowly falling in love with that girl, another pressure was growing inside me.

If I wanted to leave the country, I had to work harder than ever and save money. But at the same time, there was my mother — the woman who loved me deeply, quietly, without conditions. And I kept asking myself: How can I leave her?

At that time, we were all living in the same house.

My parents lived there, along with my two younger sisters, my younger brother, and me. Two of my brothers older than me were also still single and living at home. Three other brothers older than me were already married and living separately, each in his own house. I also had two older sisters who were married and living with their husbands.

For a while, my oldest brother — the first child of my parents — lived with us too, together with his wife and their children: two sons and two daughters. Space was tight, but we were used to that kind of life.

The living room was our bedroom.

Four single brothers — including me — and one of my nephews, the oldest one, slept there. He grew up with us. We slept on rugs, using blankets and pillows in both winter and summer. No beds. No private rooms. No wardrobes. One of my brothers who was working bought himself a wardrobe. My younger brother and I shared a small drawer. It was tiny, but better than leaving our clothes on the floor. We didn't expect much from life. We were used to "enough."

Two of my single brothers worked extremely hard. One was a security guard at the oil refinery. The other was a painter. Later, my father helped him find a permanent full-time job through a friend, but even then he continued painting in his free time to earn extra money. He worked relentlessly — his whole life. Even now, as I write this and he is officially retired, he still paints to support his family and help his sons prepare for marriage.

Eventually, my father and my older married brothers decided it was time for those two single brothers to get married. The brides were chosen from within our relatives. My brothers did not choose for themselves — the decision was made for them.

One of those nights stays with me forever.

My brother, the painter, cried on his wedding night.

Have you ever seen a man cry on the day he is supposed to be happiest? He cried because he obeyed my father. Because he respected him. Because he didn't want to break his word — even though his heart wasn't ready.

The wedding was held the traditional way, in our home and our neighbors' homes. Men and women celebrated separately. Men were not allowed in the women's gathering. Only the groom could enter to dance with his bride, his sisters, his mother, and close female relatives. Our neighbors opened their houses generously — even to people they didn't know. This was common in those days. Not everyone could afford a wedding hall.

Food was cooked at home by people known for their cooking. Hundreds were fed — sometimes more. Lamb, chicken, rice, potatoes, sweets, fruit, tea coffee. For relatives coming from far cities, hospitality started days earlier– breakfast, lunch, and dinner, like a small restaurant run by family. My father chose to marry both brothers on the same night to reduce costs. One celebration instead of two. A few days after the wedding, both brothers moved out and started their own lives. The living room felt larger. Only three of us remained sleeping there: me, my younger brother, and my nephew.

Later, my oldest brother– who had been living in a small bedroom with his wife and children– also moved out. He had problems with his eyes and couldn't work properly. He survived on small government benefits. He was a kind man, gentle and accepting of life, even with its limits.

Years passed in that house — the one we moved into after the war.

When my father finally bought it from the owner, we decided to demolish it and rebuild. It was an old one-story house: a living room, two bedrooms, a kitchen-dining room, one bathroom, and a toilet separated in the front yard. To enter the house, you passed through the yard first.

We moved temporarily into my cousin's empty house by renting it. Then, day after day, we returned to our old home and demolished it with our own hands — pickaxes, shovels, simple tools. Slowly, piece by piece, the house came down.

As I stood there, breaking walls that had held so many memories, I didn't know yet that my own life was also preparing for another collapse — and another rebuild.

Rebuilding, Work, Love, and the Choice to Leave

I started working with other people's cars whenever I could. Sometimes I made some money, sometimes nothing at all, especially when the owners needed their cars for their own lives. At the same time, we were knocking down our house, and during that period I could not work as a driver at all. That meant no income.

We demolished the house brick by brick with our own hands — no machines, no equipment. Just pickaxes, shovels, and long days of physical exhaustion. It took a long time.

Later, my father made an agreement with a builder who was also a distant relative. The plan was to build a new house, this time with two floors. The builder brought two of his own workers, and my brothers and I worked alongside them every day to finish the house faster. After about a year and a half, the house was completed, and we finally moved back into our own home.

When I didn't have a car to drive, I worked at the small kiosk selling cigarettes and daily items. When I found a car, I worked again as a driver. I kept moving between these two lives, trying to save money — especially for a passport.

Around that time, there was a business opportunity some people used. Wealthy traders would take people like us on a short trip to the UAE for three days. They paid for the flight, hotel, and food, but they used our passports to buy large quantities of goods. They made big profits back home, while we were only allowed to buy small personal items. It was a smart system for them — small cost, large profit.

That was how I traveled to Dubai for the first time in my twenties.

Everything there felt different. Tall buildings. Order. Safety. Freedom. People obeyed the law, but they were not suffocated by it. You could practice religion freely, or not at all. You could live without fear.

Freedom was the most important thing to me. When you don't have it, it feels like you are being slowly killed over time.

I didn't want to go back, but I had no choice. The visa was short, I had no money, no connections, and the people who brought us needed our passports to clear their goods. After three days, we returned.

It felt like leaving heaven and going back to hell.

That short trip stayed in my memory forever.

Around the same time, the love I had for that girl came to an end.

One day, while I was sitting at the kiosk, a close friend and neighbor came to talk to me. He knew how I felt about her. He told me something I wasn't ready to hear — that she was engaged to someone else.

Later, I found out it was true. She hadn't done anything wrong. Her family would never have accepted me, and she didn't want to hurt me by telling me the truth directly. When I saw her that day, it ended everything for me.

I remember her as a good girl, and I remember the beautiful moments we shared — even if they were only eye contact from a distance. Sometimes love exists within boundaries that never allow it to grow.

That day, I smoked my first cigarette.

I didn't continue smoking after that — not then. That cigarette reminded me of something from my army days, when many trainers smoked and used drugs in crowded sleeping rooms. I stayed away from it back then because I only wanted to finish my service and leave without problems.

After the end of that love, I returned to my routine.

Driving when I had work. Standing behind the kiosk when I didn't. Working long hours, sometimes through the night. I loved driving, but no matter how hard I worked, I couldn't save enough money to buy my own car.

At the same time, I was taking care of my mother — taking her to doctors, hospitals, and sometimes to other cities for better treatment. And through all of this, my mind was constantly searching for one thing: a way out of the country.

Chapter 5

The First Escape

Eventually, I decided to leave illegally.

I didn't have enough money to leave legally, and I saw no future if I stayed. I planned to cross the border on foot. A cousin of mine, one year younger than me, asked to come along. He hadn't completed military service yet, and he believed it would be safer if we went together.

We packed a few clothes and the little money we had and traveled city to city until we reached the last town near the border.

Crossing from the main border point was impossible — it was heavily guarded. Barbed wire, soldiers, and shoot-to-kill authority. We searched for alternative routes, but every option was dangerous.

Eventually, we moved toward another border — the one near the area where I had spent part of my army service.

In a small town near the border, we met a local man while he was working outside his house. He knew the land. He knew the risks.

He asked us questions:

Did we know anyone on the other side?

Did someone help us?

Did we understand what awaited us?

The answer was no to everything.

He warned us clearly. The desert. The mountains. Armed patrols hidden in the dark. Death by thirst. Prison if caught. I accepted his advice and wanted to turn back. My cousin did not. I couldn't leave him alone.

Before continuing, I told him the truth:

We might be killed.

We might be imprisoned.

We might disappear.

We agreed on one thing — if caught, we would say we were lost.

That night, we started walking through the mountains.

After hours, a voice shouted, "Stop," and a gun was pointed at us. We were arrested.

They blindfolded us, handcuffed us, and took us to a military post. They separated us. I was questioned first. I repeated our agreement: We got lost.
They beat me and sent me back to a cell.
Later, they took my cousin.

A soldier quietly told me the truth afterward: my cousin had told them everything.
In that moment, I understood something deeply and painfully — I had chosen the wrong person to cross the border with.

When they brought me back for questioning, they already "knew everything." There was no point lying anymore. I told the truth to stop the pain. But that was only the beginning. They didn't believe our intentions. Everything was against us

— my army background, his lack of service, the language difference, the location.

After they knew the truth, everything changed.

They transferred us to the capital city of that state and sent us to a main prison there.

But the way they did it is something I will never forget.

They treated us like animals.

They put us on the back of an army ute, blindfolded, handcuffed, and covered with a blanket so no one could see us during the journey. Our only crime was trying to cross the border illegally. Nothing else. But they did not treat us like human beings. And the fact that our mother language was not the main language of the country made everything worse.

When we arrived at the prison, they placed us in a large room with other prisoners. Around thirty men in one space. There was barely enough room to sit or lie down on the floor. A single toilet inside the room that was shared by everyone. They gave us food, but only by name — it did not resemble food.

After some time, they transferred us again. From that moment on, I did not see my cousin, and he did not see me, until we met later in court.

The days passed very slowly. My mind was constantly with my family, especially my mother. I kept thinking about what would happen when they found out where I was. Each day felt like a year.

Then they sent me to solitary confinement. No going outside. No sunlight. No way to know whether it was day or night. I saw no one. Even when they brought food through a small window in the door, I had to wear a blindfold so I could not see who they were. Inside the sell, I noticed marks on the wall left by prisoners before me — lines counting the days. I chose not to mark anything. I had no choice but to accept where I was and endure it.

The worst moment came during interrogation.

They made me stand on an empty 200-liter barrel, blindfolded
and handcuffed. Then they removed the barrel and hung me
from the ceiling by my wrists. My hands were tied tightly with a
rope. The pain started almost immediately — a burning
sensation in both wrists that made me feel as if my arms would
be torn from my body.

While I was hanging there, they questioned me and punched
me in the stomach.

They asked which group I was working with, what my position
was, what we were writing against the government, who I was
connected to, what our next move was. Questions about things
I had never even thought about in my life.

Why did they do this?

Because they did not believe we were simply trying to leave the
country.

Because I had completed my military service in that region.

Because my cousin had not completed his service.

Because of our language.

Everything was against me, and they saw me as the reason.

I kept screaming that we were not part of any group, that we were not against the government, that we only wanted to leave the country. But we had no power. They did. And no one knew where we were or what they were doing to us.

I will not write how long I stayed in prison.

Time there loses meaning anyway.

Later, I found out that they did not treat my cousin the same way they treated me. And honestly, I was relieved. During the torture, all I could think about was hoping they would not do to him what they were doing to me.

The day finally came when we saw each other again — in court. We were brought there blindfolded and handcuffed again, but this time not like animals.

We were released.

But freedom came with a price.

I left the court with a criminal record in the country where I was born — a record for something I did not do. That record followed me everywhere. I could not work in any job that required a police check. I lost my passport. I could no longer leave the country legally.

The next day, they returned our belongings and sent us out of the prison.

I felt both happy and empty. I did not know what to do next.

When we returned home, we told our families the truth. There was anger, disappointment, and judgment — especially toward me. But I learned one thing clearly: I would never again do something like this with my cousin, or with anyone else. If I ever tried again, I would do it alone.

What followed was quieter, but heavier.

I was free, yet nothing felt free anymore. I carried the weight of what had happened inside me every day. The prison walls were gone, but something invisible had replaced them. I had returned to the same streets, the same faces, the same routines — but I was not the same person.

The criminal record followed me everywhere.

Any job that required a police check was now closed to me. Any official path forward was blocked. Even the passport — the one document that symbolized escape — was taken from me. Legally, I was trapped.

I had been punished not only for what I tried to do, but for who I was suspected of being.

People looked at me differently. Some avoided me. Some judged silently. Some spoke openly. And some pretended nothing had happened, which somehow hurt even more. I learned quickly that once a label is placed on you, removing it is almost impossible — even when it is undeserved.

Inside my family, things were not easy either. Their fear came out as anger. Their worry turned into blame. I understood them, even when it hurt. They had imagined losing me — to prison, to death, or to disappearance — and fear does not speak gently.

But the hardest part was my mother.

Every time I looked at her, I felt the weight of what I had put her through. The nights she didn't know where I was. The days she waited without answers. No punishment I received from the system felt heavier than that.

Life slowly returned to routine. I worked where I could. I helped at home. I stood behind the kiosk again. I drove when there was work. From the outside, it looked like nothing had changed.

Inside, everything had.

I no longer believed in luck.

I no longer trusted easy paths.

And I no longer believed that freedom comes without cost.

Yet the desire to leave did not die.

If anything, it became sharper — more focused, more patient. I stopped rushing. I stopped trusting words. I stopped sharing plans. I learned to observe, to wait, and to prepare silently.

That failed escape did not end my journey.

It reshaped it.

And although I didn't know it then, that chapter — painful as it was — became the foundation for everything that came after.

Before I met the woman who later became my wife, there was another chapter — quieter, shorter, but meaningful.

I fell in love again.

One day, while I was driving through the city looking for passengers, I saw two women standing on the side of the road, waiting for a taxi. I stopped and asked where they were going. They said to the next city — only about twenty minutes away. The two cities were almost connected, but each had its own name and identity.

I agreed, and they got into the car.

From the very first moment, my eyes were drawn to one of them. When she sat in the back seat beside the other woman, I began to notice her through the rear-view mirror. I could feel her looking at me too. I was shy. I didn't know how to start a conversation, and for several minutes we drove in silence.

Then, finally, I spoke.

I don't remember exactly how the conversation began, but slowly we started talking. I learned that she wasn't from our city — she was visiting, a guest of the other woman, and they were relatives.

After a short while, she surprised me. She said, calmly and clearly, that she would only talk to me if I truly intended to marry her one day.

Her honesty shook me — in a good way.

I told her the truth: that if I wanted to know her, it was only because I was thinking of her as a future partner, not as something temporary. She told me she felt the same. She had felt something from the beginning too.

At that time, we didn't have mobile phones. There were no numbers to exchange, no messages to send. They went on to the other city to spend the day — walking, eating, enjoying time by the river.

Before they got out of the car, I asked if they would like me to come back later and take them home at a time they chose. They agreed.

After dropping them off, I returned to work — but my body was driving while my mind was somewhere else. I kept thinking about her eyes, her smile, her words, and the way everything had felt so sudden and sincere.

When the time came to pick them up, I arrived early. I didn't want them to wait for me — not even for a moment.

After I picked them up, I drove them back to their home in our city. During the days that followed, while she was still there, I saw her a few more times. Before she returned to her own city, we exchanged addresses. She also gave me a phone number — not her own, but one belonging to a close relative. She told me that if I called that number, I could ask to speak with her, whether the same day or another day.

At that time, we didn't have a phone at home. So if we wanted to talk, we had to go to places that offered phone services — small offices where you gave them a number, and they connected the call for you. Other times, we wrote letters to each other and sent them by post.

Both ways were beautiful.

Talking to her, or waiting for a letter from her, gave me a feeling of fullness — as if I already had everything I needed, just by knowing she existed and that we shared something real.

The next time she visited our city, she told me she wanted to come with her mother to visit my family at our home. I told her it was completely fine. Before that visit, I spoke to my mother and my sisters so they would understand what was happening. Until then, they hadn't known anything about her.

My father was at home too, but I didn't tell him the truth. I knew he wouldn't accept it — at least not in the beginning — and I didn't feel it was necessary. I asked my mother that if he asked, she should say that they were the mother and sister of a friend of mine from the army, visiting us from another city. Of course, that wasn't the truth — but at that time, it felt like the only way.

They came and visited us. The meeting was short, polite, and calm. But even in that brief time, I felt something heavy in my chest. I had a strong feeling that her mother would never accept me as a partner or future husband for her daughter.

After they left, time passed.

A few months into our relationship, I decided to visit her in her city. I asked her first if it was okay — if she wanted to see me. She said yes. She even told me that I could stay overnight at their house, and that her mother had agreed.

So I went.

Her city was far — about ten hours away by bus. As I traveled, I carried hope, fear, and excitement all together. I didn't know what awaited me there, but I knew one thing clearly: I was walking into something important, something that would stay with me, no matter how it ended.

Chapter 6

A Love That Could Not Stay

I arrived in her city knowing something important already:

She lived alone with her mother. Her father had passed away a few years earlier because of diabetes. She had no brothers or sisters. She was her mother's only child — her entire world. Because of that, her mother watched her future carefully, protectively, the way only a parent with one child can.

After a few taxi rides, I found their house.

They opened their door to me with the same warmth we had shown them before. Their hospitality was honest and respectful. I felt welcomed — not as a stranger, but as a guest they trusted.

When night came, I didn't want to stay and sleep in their house. I felt it would be more appropriate to go to a hotel. But they refused. They told me they knew what kind of person I was. So they prepared a bed for me in the living room, where I would sleep alone, while they went to their bedroom.

Before sleeping, she came and sat next to me.

We talked.

That moment remains one of the purest moments of my life. There was no touch, no crossing of lines — only words, silence, and presence. I felt at peace. I felt closeness. I felt something deep and rare.

And yet, at the same time, I felt disappointment settling quietly inside me.

Her mother knew what I did for a living. I was a driver.

It was not a stable job. Not a stable income. And in her eyes, not the future she wanted for her daughter.

I understood her.

Being kind, respectful, and sincere is not always enough to be chosen as a life partner. Love alone does not erase fear about the future. Her mother wanted safety, certainty, and stability for the only child she had left in this world.

She had no power over her mother's decision — and she was hurt by it, just as I was. But we both knew what it meant.

This relationship had to end.

That night, I did not want time to move forward.

I did not want her to stand up and leave the room. I did not want that moment to become a memory.

Even now, years later, I still remember her.

I don't know where she is. I don't know how her life turned out — whether she married, whether she had children, whether she was happy. I tried to find her, not to return, not to disturb her life — only to know that she is well. But I never did.

I returned home carrying disappointment quietly inside me.

And I never saw her again.

Chapter 7

Work, Survival, and the Turning Point

A Year of Work, a Night of Fire, and a Body That Spoke

I returned to our city with pain in my heart and no clear direction. I didn't know what to do next, only that I couldn't stay still.

I was still in contact with a close friend I had met during my army service. After many conversations, he told me there might be a chance for me to work at a privately owned company where he was employed as a lathe operator. I agreed immediately. When I asked him about accommodation, he told me the company had a room inside the factory for workers who came from other cities. I would be sharing it with others, but it would be enough.

I waited until he confirmed the interview. When he did, I traveled from my city to the capital. The factory itself was about an hour outside the capital, in a smaller city nearby. My friend had also moved there from his hometown to be closer to work.

The company specialized in manufacturing firefighting equipment. I started as a general laborer, doing whatever was asked of me. I knew nothing about the job at first, but slowly I learned. Over time, they trusted me with more responsibility.

My main task became working with a drill press. I stood in the same spot for most of the day, drilling parts for firefighting equipment. Winter came, and it was harsh — cold, snowy, and unforgiving. At night, I slept in a small room inside the factory with four other workers. The company also employed a night security guard to protect the warehouse.

The guard was a foreign worker. His salary was low, but it was still better than nothing for him and his family.

Some weekends, my friend invited me to his home. His house was less than an hour away by car. On the last working day of the week, we would travel together, stay two nights, eat proper food, rest, and then return to work at the start of the new week.

I worked there for nearly a year.

One night, everything changed.

As usual, we were sleeping in the company room. The warehouse was locked, and the security guard was on duty. I woke up in the middle of the night to use the bathroom. The bathroom was outside the sleeping room, and from there you could see the large warehouse gate.

At first, nothing seemed unusual. But as I came out of the bathroom, I noticed a utility vehicle parked near the warehouse and several men loading equipment into it.

For a moment, I didn't understand what I was seeing. Then they saw me.

They began rushing, trying to escape. Without thinking, I ran back to the room, grabbed a heavy wooden stick I kept under my blanket, and shouted loudly to wake the others:

"Thieves!"

Barefoot, I ran outside after them.

They had guns. I didn't.

If they had decided to shoot, I wouldn't be alive today. But they weren't killers — they were thieves. They jumped into the vehicle and drove toward the main gate, which was already open.

When I reached the gate, I saw the security guard tied up, blindfolded, bleeding, and crying on the ground. We hadn't heard him because the gate was far from our sleeping area.

By the time the others arrived, I had already untied him.

The thieves escaped, but my waking up had stopped them from emptying the entire warehouse before morning.

The police were called that night. The next day, management arrived and saw the damage. Many people immediately suspected the security guard, believing he had organized the robbery. I couldn't accept that accusation without proof.

There were no cameras, no evidence — only suspicion, made heavier because he was a foreigner.

The police questioned me as well, since I was the one who saw the thieves first and chased them. I told the truth, exactly as it happened, from the moment I woke up to the moment I found the guard tied on the ground.

Despite the lack of evidence, the guard was dismissed. Later, the company hired another guard — this time with a large security dog.

Life at work returned to normal.

But my body didn't.

I began feeling pain in both knees. Sitting became difficult. Standing for long hours was even worse. Still, I continued working.

I had learned to endure pain without complaint.

Eventually, the pain became impossible to ignore. I spoke to the manager and asked if I could occasionally sit for one or two minutes during the day. He agreed, knowing how hard I worked.

A few days later, I realized even that wasn't enough.

I went to see a specialist in the city. After listening to me, he asked for a colored X-ray. When he saw the results, he was shocked.

The first thing he asked was my age.

I was still in my twenties — around twenty-five, maybe younger.

"You have arthritis in both knees," he said.

He asked about my job. When I told him I stood all day, every day, he shook his head.

"This usually happens to people in their sixties or seventies," he said. "It can happen earlier, but not at your age."

His advice was clear and firm:

- Leave this job immediately.

- Rest.

- Strengthen your knees with exercise.

"No medication will fix this," he told me. "And surgery is not suitable for you at this age."

I listened.

After speaking with my manager and explaining my condition, I left the job.

But I didn't go home.

The Road That Wasn't Mine

About two hours from the capital was a city where one of my uncles lived. When the war began, he had moved there with his family, and many of his children were born after that move. His oldest son was a few years younger than me, but we were close — more like friends than cousins.

Before leaving my job at the firefighting equipment factory, I spoke to him. He knew I could drive, and he told me about a man who owned a car and was looking for a driver. The owner was very careful and didn't trust just anyone with his vehicle, but my cousin believed that if he introduced me personally, the man might accept.

I went to my uncle's house first. After visiting and spending some time together, we arranged a meeting with the car owner.

He was a kind man, much older than me — at least twenty or twenty-five years older. He had a large family, with both sons and daughters, something I learned later while working with him. We agreed on a percentage-based arrangement, and he allowed me to keep the car overnight since he didn't need it daily. Whenever he needed it, he said, he would let me know.

I started working by taking passengers from that city to the capital, a journey of about two hours by car. At first, it wasn't easy. I didn't know the roads well, especially inside the capital. It took several trips before I became familiar with the main routes, though never all of them.

I woke up early every morning, around five o'clock, and went to the usual spot where people gathered to travel to the capital. After dropping them off, I searched for passengers heading back toward my uncle's city. On busy days, I managed two trips each way. Three was rare.

Once a week, I met the car owner, gave him his share, and kept mine.

At night, I slept at my uncle's house. It was a two-story home. I slept upstairs with his two sons, mostly with the older one. My uncle, his wife, and his daughters slept downstairs.

They treated me well, especially my uncle's wife. She liked me very much — so much, in fact, that she hoped I might one day marry one of her daughters. I respected her greatly, but I didn't feel the same way, and I knew I had to be careful.

After about three months, I realized this situation couldn't continue.

I was working on another man's car, living in a city that wasn't my own, and sleeping in a house with several young women. I knew how people talked, how relatives thought, and how quickly intentions could be misunderstood. Even if nothing improper was happening, the situation itself was not right.

So I decided to leave and return home.

Before that, there were times when the car owner asked me to drive him and his family when I had no passengers. Once, he asked me to take them to the capital to visit a friend. We agreed that I would return at night to pick them up after he called me an hour beforehand.

That day, his daughter — who was in her final year of high school — was with them. I had already noticed that she liked me. I could see it in her eyes. But because I was driving her father's car, I felt that even acknowledging this was a betrayal.

On the way to the capital, she sat in the back seat. Every time I checked the rearview mirror, I saw her watching me.

On the way back, she moved closer, sitting directly behind my seat. She pressed her knees against the back of it, gently but deliberately, trying to provoke a reaction. I felt it clearly.

I said nothing.

I did nothing.

I controlled myself until we reached home.

When I later returned the car and told the owner I was leaving, he asked me why. I explained honestly: it wasn't right for me to stay longer in my uncle's house, especially with daughters there, and I didn't know how long I could live that way.

What he said next surprised me.

"Then come live with us," he said. "I'll give you a furnished room. Work with my car. This will be your home."

The moment he said that, his daughter came to my mind.

I knew I couldn't accept it. Living in his house, knowing his daughter's feelings, would be a deeper betrayal — even if he trusted me completely.

I thanked him sincerely and refused.

He repeated the offer more than once. When he finally saw that my decision wouldn't change, he said something I never forgot:

"Anytime you want to come back and work with my car, don't hesitate. My home will always be open for you."

I thanked him again, from my heart.

Then I left.

That was the last time I ever saw him.

Chapter 8

The Second Escape

I went back home, knowing very well what was waiting for me there — disappointment. I also knew that if I stayed without work, I would face the same pressure and criticism from my father as before. I didn't want to return, but at the same time, I had no other choice.

The kiosk was now managed by my older brother and his eldest son. Sometimes I helped them, but I wasn't working there regularly. I also couldn't find a car to work as a driver.

At the same time, my mind never stopped searching for a way out of the country.

I had a close friend — our neighbor — who told me that some people left the country by hiding on large cargo ships traveling to European countries, or even Canada. But nothing about that path was simple. Some ships would take people for large sums of money, far beyond what I had. Another option was to work near a port and try to leave from there — but even that was extremely difficult.

After searching and asking around, I learned that most people who tried this route went to one of the country's major ports. Ships from many parts of the world arrived there to unload goods and load new cargo before returning to their countries.

The first challenge was entering the port itself.

Access required official work — either directly employed at the port or working under a contractor. Each ship that arrived needed laborers to unload and reload cargo. Contractors brought workers, issued temporary IDs, and assigned them to specific ships. Once the job was done, the workers were dismissed.

For those who wanted to escape, this system created a dangerous opportunity.

The idea was to enter the port as a worker, get onto a ship, and find a place to hide during loading — unnoticed. Food and water were critical. One had to survive not only the loading days, but also the time it took for the ship to leave port and exit border waters. Sometimes that alone took weeks. The longer one stayed hidden, the safer it was to reveal oneself later to the ship's crew.

I packed a small bag with a few clothes — more than I needed, as it turned out. Later, I sent some of them back home with a friend. But at that moment, I believed I was leaving for good.

The port was about eighteen hours away by bus. I bought a ticket using money I had saved from my job at the firefighting equipment factory and from the car work I had done while living near my uncle.

Only one person knew what I was planning — my younger brother. He was four years younger than me, and we shared a deep bond and many memories. We decided not to tell anyone else. My first escape attempt had already ended in prison and a criminal record. We couldn't risk that again.

Even my brother was tired of the life we were living, but he hadn't decided to leave yet.

I told my family — especially my mother — that I was returning to work at the same factory with my friend. She worried constantly about me, so this lie was easier for her to accept. No one asked further questions.

I left alone.

When I arrived at the port city, I got off the bus near the port itself. On the edge of the desert, at the entrance to the city, I saw dozens of tents. They were filled with men — port workers. Some had jobs; others were waiting.

 When there was no work, they stayed there, waiting for contractors to come when a new ship arrived. I began asking questions quietly, looking for the man whose name I had been given.

After some time, I found him.

When I told him I was from the same city as he was, he looked at me differently — with familiarity. He said they weren't working at the moment, but if a job came up, he would take me with them into the port.

So I waited.

He asked one of his brothers to show me which tent to go to. I followed him, and inside that tent I found several men from my own city. We became friends quickly — the kind of friendship that forms fast when people share the same hardship.

Soon I realized that most of the men working at the port were casual workers, not full-time employees. They came to earn money because the pay was good — the job was extremely hard — and at the same time, if an opportunity to leave the country appeared, they would take it. If not, they worked, saved what they could, and returned home until another chance came. Some were there only to work and support their families. Others were quietly waiting for an escape.

Life in the tents was brutal.

There were no bathrooms. We used the desert.

There was no running water. We carried a large container — about twenty liters — walking long distances to fetch water for drinking, cooking, and washing. Showering was rare, only if there was enough water left. Life felt primitive, like living centuries in the past.

After a few days, I finally entered the port for work on a large ship. It wasn't from a country that accepted refugees — even if I reached it, it wouldn't save me — but we had no choice. Our money was almost gone.

While working on that ship, I met a man from my city who had been there two or three months before me. He was married and wanted to return home to see his family. I asked him if he could take my extra clothes with him and deliver them to my family, just to let them know I was alive and well.

He agreed.

But a misunderstanding followed — one that would later destroy my escape.

After he left, I continued working. A few days later, after about forty-five days without contact, I decided to call my family. We didn't have a phone at home, but one of my brothers lived nearby and did. I left the port, went to a public phone office, and called.

They were worried — especially my mother. I told them where I was and that I was working. I didn't notice that my brother was writing everything down on a piece of paper. My only intention was to let my mother know I was alive, because I knew her heart would not rest without hearing my voice.

What I didn't know was what had already happened.

When my friend delivered my clothes, one of my sisters opened the door. He gave her the bag and said, "These are your brother's clothes," then left. Nothing more.

She misunderstood.

She thought I was dead.

When my mother heard that, she cried constantly. She believed she had lost me.

When I called, my brother didn't tell me the full truth. He only said, "Mom is very worried about you. Please call again tomorrow so she can talk to you." I agreed.

The next day I called again and spoke to my mother. Even then, she didn't fully believe I was alive.

I returned to work.

Until one day, while I was loading the ship, I suddenly saw my younger brother standing there.

We ran to each other. We hugged. We kissed each other. I was shocked and happy at the same time. I couldn't understand how he had found me — in such a huge port, on this exact ship.

Later I realized the truth: during my first call, without noticing, I had given my location to my other brother.

When my younger brother saw my condition — dirty, exhausted, injured — his face changed. A few days earlier, I slipped while loading iron beams. We had no safety shoes. My foot landed on the edge of the metal, slicing the sole badly. It bled heavily, but I wrapped it and kept working. I couldn't afford to lose the job.

Seeing me like that broke him.

He said, "Brother, let's go back. You don't deserve this. If I had known it was this hard, I would never have let you come."

I didn't react — until he mentioned our mother.

"She's crying every day. She still doesn't believe you're alive. Seeing your clothes destroyed her."

That was it.

I said goodbye to the friends I had made. I left the ship. I left the port.

I returned home — not because the path was closed, but because my heart couldn't move forward while my mother believed she had buried her son.

The second escape ended there — not with chains or prison, but with love, fear, and a mother's tears.

Chapter 9

Building a Family

Choices, Silence, and the Weight of Responsibility

After I returned home, I no longer felt that I belonged to that city or to that life. There was no freedom, and the government laws were restrictive and unforgiving. My older brother was still running the small kiosk, but one day the council staff arrived. Without warning, they lifted the kiosk—everything inside it—and loaded it onto a truck. They took it to the council center.

The kiosk was small: one meter wide, two meters long, and about one and a half meters high. It did not block the road or disturb pedestrians. Many people in the city survived the same way. No one complained. But the authorities didn't care about people's lives. They made things harder every day.

Later, we followed them and paid a fine to get the kiosk back, but we were no longer allowed to place it in the same spot. When there is no work, people try anything to survive. If people had real jobs with decent salaries, no one would choose to stand in the streets all day just to make a living.

I returned to driving passengers. This time, I worked through a taxi office. People called two phone numbers, and at least fifteen to twenty drivers were available at any time, day or night. We took turns. When you returned to the depot, you waited until your turn came again—unless the city was busy, when sometimes there were no drivers left and calls kept coming.

For someone driving their own car, it wasn't bad. For someone working with someone else's car, it was hard. Twenty percent of every job went to the taxi office. From what remained, thirty percent was mine. The rest went to the car owner. I was working, but barely for myself. Still, it was better than sitting at home.

Some nights I didn't go home at all. I stayed at the taxi office as the night driver. The city would quiet down after eleven, sometimes midnight, and one driver stayed until morning while someone answered the phones.

One day, it was my turn to pick up a passenger from an orphanage. It was my first time going there. I waited a few seconds, and then I saw a woman come out and sit in the back seat of my car.

We greeted each other, and I asked where she wanted to go. I knew the area but not the exact house, so I started driving. I felt something toward her and decided to speak honestly. I told her I would like to know her—if she was not in a relationship.

She answered clearly. She said she was divorced and had a daughter. She said if I wanted to know her, it would only be with the intention of marriage. She was not interested in short-term relationships.

I respected her honesty. I thought to myself: what is the difference between a woman who has never married and a woman who has lived, married, and divorced? Even a girl becomes a woman one day. Everyone carries a past. Hers was no different from mine.

So I accepted her condition. We talked the entire way to her home. We agreed to see each other again. The next day, I picked her up for work, and after that, whenever she needed a ride, I was there.

I fell in love. Slowly, I forgot my plans to leave the country. I began thinking about marriage.

But it was not simple. I knew my family might not accept that I marry a divorced woman with a child. I didn't know how to tell them. I also couldn't go alone to ask for her hand; traditions required my father to be with me.

One day, I told my father. His answer was a clear no. He said there were many girls, and I chose a divorced woman with a child. He refused to go with me. I begged him, but he didn't change his mind.

My family found out. My mother stayed silent. My sisters only wanted to see me happy. My brothers tried to change my mind, but they saw I was serious. One brother strongly disagreed.

Even now, remembering those days hurts.

I told my brothers I didn't care about her past. This was my decision. Right or wrong, I would carry the consequences.

Three of my brothers and one of my uncles agreed to come with me to her parents' house. Her parents accepted me. After many discussions, everything was agreed.

Later, my brothers spoke to my father again and again until he finally agreed to hold a wedding ceremony at our home, like the others.

On my wedding night, I wasn't happy. One of my brothers didn't attend. I felt judged—by relatives, neighbors, and friends. No one said anything out loud, but I could see it in their eyes.

That night felt more like a death than a celebration.

Still, one thing kept me standing. Before marrying her, I promised to respect her, love her, and never hurt her. I promised nothing financially, because I didn't know what life would give me. She accepted that.

After the wedding, we lived in one room at my parents' house. A few days later, her daughter joined us. She was respectful, and my family liked her. Later, one of my brothers moved out of the second floor, and I moved in. For the first time, we had a small but complete home.

I continued working as a taxi driver. After one year, my first son was born.

I was very happy. He stayed in my arms constantly. As he grew, we became inseparable. My family loved him deeply.

Then something changed. My wife began hitting him. He was only about a year old. My mother and sisters tried to stop her. She became angrier. Conflicts grew.

One day, her mother came to our house. Suddenly my wife started screaming and disrespecting my mother. I lost control and slapped her once. My parents left. Her mother left. Later, my father told me to leave the house.

I had nowhere to go.

One of my brothers took me in. He let us live in his house for almost a year without rent. I worked to cover daily expenses.

Later, my younger brother introduced me to a networking business in the capital. I borrowed money to join. I worked day and night. After forty days, I received a call: another fight between my wife and my family.

Everything felt against me.

I decided to move to the capital with my wife and children. Life there became harder. The business collapsed. Money ran out.

While the networking business was falling apart and I was still living in the capital, my wife gave birth to my second son. Both of them were unwell—especially my newborn. There were moments when I truly believed we might lose him.

They stayed in the hospital for two weeks. During that time, I was alone, taking care of my first son, who was only eighteen months old. Every day, I went back and forth to the hospital to check on my wife and my newborn son. There was no family with us, no support, no one else to help.

After two long weeks, the doctors finally discharged them. We returned home together, exhausted, afraid, and uncertain about what tomorrow would bring.

We moved between houses. There was violence. Humiliation. Silence.

Finally, with nothing left, I decided to leave the country.

I made passports for my wife and sons. I made a fake one for myself. We told no one. Her daughter had to be returned to her father through court.

Before leaving, I went to my parents' house. I kissed their hands and said goodbye.

A few days later, with fear in my chest and my children beside me, I crossed the border with a fake passport.

And that was only the beginning.

Chapter 10

Waiting in Syria

After passing the border safely and traveling for three days by bus, we arrived in the country where I planned to apply for refugee status. I was with my wife and my two sons. The younger one was eight months old, and the older one was two years old.

Before leaving my country, I had gathered some information about people from my city who had been living there for a few years. After asking around, I found one of them. He was working with his two sons and living with his wife and children. He was a kind man. He helped me by introducing me to someone who assisted refugees in finding accommodation, depending on their budget.

Because I didn't know how long the refugee process would take, and because the money I had with me had to last until I found work, I had to be extremely careful. Based on what I could afford, we rented a small one-bedroom underground apartment.

A few days later, we went to the UNHCR and applied for refugee status. The country we were living in did not accept refugees permanently, but it allowed us to stay temporarily until our case was processed and a third country accepted us for resettlement. That was the beginning of our life as refugees.

At that time, I believed the process would take no more than one year. I was wrong.

After applying, I immediately started looking for work. The money I had would last only two or three months at most. I found a job through two men from my country, but I left after a few days because I didn't like the shop owner's behavior. His behavior was aggressive, and he was constantly swearing. I then found another job in a fabric store owned by four brothers who had two shops facing each other. I worked in the bigger shop.

At that time, I was thirty-three years old — the same age I was when I left my hometown. Until the moment I am writing this book, I have never returned.

My daily routine was exhausting. I woke up at 4 a.m., arrived at the shop by 5 a.m., worked until noon, went home briefly for lunch, then returned to work until 8 or 9 p.m. Every day was the same.

During this period, my wife and I were called several times for interviews with the UNHCR. Sometimes they asked the same questions again and again. They interviewed us separately, not together, to check if our stories matched.

After about a year, I felt completely exhausted. I found another job at a shoe store.

Around that time, a close friend of mine followed me to Syria. At first, he came alone and stayed with us in our small apartment for about two months. Later, his wife and his only daughter — who was the same age as my older son — joined him. Once they arrived, we helped them find a place to rent, and they moved out.

My friend applied for refugee status just like I did. He was working in the shoe store where I later worked as well. Whenever I visited him there, the owner knew me, because he was friends with the owners of the fabric shop I used to work for.

I asked my friend to let me know if they needed another worker. The owner later told me he was planning to open a new store with his brother and wanted me to work with them. I accepted. The hours were better, and the pay was slightly higher. The fabric shop owners were upset that I left, but living abroad teaches you that survival comes before loyalty.

Even with that job, life was not easy. Rent, food, and two children were a heavy responsibility. Time passed slowly. After one and a half years, I went to the UNHCR to ask about our case. I was told that our case manager had left the country and that we needed to repeat all interviews with a new officer.

We started again from zero.

During this time, my friend received his result. He was rejected.

He was lost. His wife didn't want to stay anymore. She wanted to return to her relatives in our home country. He was working very hard, suffering, and still had no future there.

I spoke to him honestly. I told him he had two options:

Either appeal the decision and wait again, without knowing how long it would take or whether he would ever be accepted — or return home with his wife and live a life they at least understood.

In the end, they decided to return to our home country.

Watching him leave affected me deeply.

We repeated our interviews again and waited.

I left the shoe store and started working in the market. I bought socks,hand towels and bath towels, t-shirts, and singlets from wholesalers and sold them by hand, standing outside shops with a bag. It was very hard work. Some shop owners allowed us to sell because our products were different from theirs, but sometimes the council came without warning and confiscated everything.

Because I had no legal visa and was living as a refugee, I avoided any confrontation. Losing money was better than being arrested and deported.

After more than two years, our result finally came.

We were accepted as refugees.

But acceptance did not mean resettlement. We still had to wait for a country to accept us permanently.

I continued selling in the market for another year, but the council made it harder and harder. Eventually, I found a job in a hotel as a tour leader for visitors from my country. They stayed for a week and returned home. Because they couldn't speak the local language, they needed someone to guide them. This was the best job I had there — more responsibility, but better income.

Over four years, we moved several times. Our last place was the best: a one-bedroom apartment with a proper living room, kitchen, and bathroom.

After nearly four years, the UNHCR informed us that we had to leave. War had started, and our safety was no longer guaranteed. There were thousands of refugees, and UNHCR could no longer protect us.

That country was Syria.

With help from a friend I had met while selling clothes in the market, I obtained a fake passport again and left Syria for Indonesia. I had saved money for emergencies, and that money saved us once more.

Those four years in Syria were not easy. It is easy to say "four years," but living every single day not knowing what tomorrow holds, in a foreign country, with a wife and two children, is something else entirely.

I cannot write every detail. Some memories are too personal. I have written what matters most.

The worst, however, happened in Indonesia.

That story belongs to the next chapter.

Chapter 11

Indonesia – The Edge of Another Choice

After four years of living in Syria, with all its ups and downs, we finally arrived at Jakarta airport. I was hoping we would pass immigration without any problems—just as we had passed through Damascus airport, which had worried me deeply. I was afraid they might discover our passports and arrest us. But we passed through two borders safely and entered the capital city of Indonesia.

During those four years in Syria, I had always tried to save money for the worst-case scenario. That saving is what saved us. It allowed me to pay for the passports, the tickets, and a hotel in Indonesia.

After one day at the hotel, I asked the reception desk if they knew where the UNHCR office was located. They guided us, and we took a taxi there. I went with my wife and my two sons, who were now around five years old (the younger) and six and a half years old (the older).

We gave them our contact details, and they told us they would schedule an interview. I explained that we had already been refugees for four years and that we had already been accepted, but they told us that we needed to start a new process and do new interviews.

When I heard that, I felt deeply upset. I immediately thought about the four years we had spent in Syria and the possibility that we might spend the same amount of time—or even more—in Indonesia. Before going to UNHCR, I had already bought an Indonesian SIM card so they could contact us if needed.

We returned to the hotel, but I knew we couldn't stay there for long. Our money would run out sooner or later.

At the UNHCR building, I met a man who had arrived in Indonesia before us and was there that day for his interview. I started talking to him and asked about life in Indonesia and the refugee process. He told me it could take four to five years for everything to be completed. I also asked him about renting a place, and he told me that living in the capital was expensive.

He said he lived about three hours away from Jakarta and knew someone who could help me find a more affordable place to live. He gave me that man's phone number.

After returning to the hotel, I called him and explained that I was new in Indonesia and had received his number from someone at UNHCR. He spoke kindly and told me to come, saying he would help us find a place. He gave me his address, and the next morning we left the hotel and went to see him.

When we arrived, he opened his home to me and my family. Over time, we became close friends, and we still are today as I write this book. He had his own family—his wife, a son, and a young daughter. He was also applying for refugee status and had been living there for a few months.

That same day, he showed me a house for rent just twenty meters from his own home. I checked the rent and realized I could afford it with the money I had. It would allow us to stay for at least a few months. I didn't think beyond that.

I began seeing this man almost every day, and our friendship grew. I also realized that many refugees from different countries were living in the area.

When our UNHCR appointment came, we returned to Jakarta with the family. The interview was long. They asked many questions—why we left Syria, how we lived during those four years, and how we arrived in Indonesia. After the interview, we returned to the house we had rented.

Later, another friend of mine followed me from Syria. He was from the same hometown as me. I gave him a room in our house. He lived with us, ate with us, and slept there. He was single and had no one, so I tried to help him as much as I could.

By then, it was clear to me that this process could take many years again. We had already spent four years waiting in Syria. We were mentally exhausted. In Indonesia, we were not allowed to work. It was illegal for foreigners without visas, and if someone reported us, we could be imprisoned. There was no financial support, no work, and no clear future.

I started thinking constantly:

How can I survive four or five years like this?

With no work, no income, a wife, and two children?

The money I had was enough for only a few months—rent, food, basic living. It didn't include medical emergencies.

Then I discovered something important.

Many refugees in Indonesia were leaving illegally by sea to Australia. Not by real ships, but by large wooden boats floating on the ocean. I will explain more about this later.

Until then, my intention had been to complete everything legally through UNHCR and be resettled in a third country. But Indonesia was very far from Europe, the USA, and Canada . Australia was the closest.

This was all during our first month in Indonesia. Time moved very slowly.

I began asking questions—how people go to Australia, how much it costs, how long it takes, the risks, and the chances of success. Eventually, I found someone who said he could take us. I later learned there were many others involved.

I told my friend who was living with us about my decision. He said he would come with me.

I spoke to my wife. I explained that waiting another four or five years—with no guarantee—might destroy us mentally. We were already exhausted from Syria. We decided to try the ocean, like many others had done at that time. That route is now closed forever.

I found out the cost. I had exactly that amount—and a little more.

We decided to go.

I told the friend who had helped me find the house that if anything happened to us, he should contact my family overseas. I told my wife honestly that we might never arrive—that we might die in the ocean, like many families before us. Even now, I feel sorrow for those people—men, women, children, and elderly—whose stories were never told.

After one and a half months in Indonesia, the night finally came.

They took us by car for about three hours to another city. We didn't know where we were going. Then they put us in a small apartment and told us not to go outside until further notice.

After a few days, they took us by minibus—along with other people we didn't know—on an eight to nine-hour journey to the coast.

We arrived in the middle of the night.

The bus stopped. We were told to get out quickly. Carrying our small bags, I ran toward the beach with my wife, my children, and my friend—into the darkness.

Chapter 12

The Ocean

When we reached the beach in the middle of the night, we saw many other people arriving at the same time, including those who had come with us in the minibus. We were told to enter the sea and walk toward a small boat. That small boat would then transfer us to the main ship waiting farther away, because the ship itself could not come close to shore—it would get stuck in the sand.

I carried one of my sons in my arms, with a bag on my back, and held my wife's hand. My friend carried my other son. We entered the sea together and walked forward until the water reached our chests. With help from people already inside the small boat, we climbed in. From there, we were transferred to the ship.

Once we climbed onto it, we realized the truth. This was not a real ship. It was small, made of wood, and overcrowded. After everyone boarded, there was no space to move at all. People were forced to sit tightly packed together—especially women and children—unable to stand or change position.

To describe it honestly, we were transported like animals. Even animals are treated better than how we were treated that night. The ship was filled with children, young men, elderly people, and only four families, including mine.

Before the night ended and morning arrived, the ship began to move. There was no proper toilet, no proper food—nothing was normal. We had been cheated. Days earlier, they had shown us photos of a large, safe ship, but now we were already there, surrounded by people, with no way back. We had no choice but to continue.

From the beginning of my life, I never truly knew what happiness meant or what it looked like. I had always searched for freedom, even when my life was in danger. But this time, it wasn't only my life—it was the lives of my wife and my two sons.

We had already agreed to this journey before reaching this point. We had already survived eight years of war. We had lived a life where even the meaning of "life" was unclear—full of restrictions, fear, and judgment. For me, freedom meant living in a place where people are not judged by their language, ethnicity, background, or beliefs.

That is why I was not thinking about death. I was thinking about survival. About life. About responsibility—for my family.

I am writing my life in this book so that you, the reader, can learn from my experience and never be forced to live it yourself. I write so you can understand how people like me lived, how we struggled, what mistakes we made, and what hopes we carried—just to live a simple life.

This book is not fiction. It is not written to entertain or to become popular like a movie. It is written because there are lives far harder than mine—stories that never get told.

The ship moved for about one day before a hole appeared underneath it. After only a few hours at sea, our mobile phones lost signal. Panic began to spread.

The ship had two small generators that were used to pump water out and back into the ocean. On the second day, the GPS broke. Then another hole appeared. The marine cordless handset also stopped working. Panic grew stronger.

I stayed close to my wife and sons, protecting them as much as I could. But when I saw the holes getting larger and more water flooding in, I knew sitting was no longer an option. The generators stopped working completely. It was only the second day.

My friend—who had worked on fishing boats back home and had some experience—went to help the captain. The captain was there with only his son, responsible for 110 people on a ship so small that no one could move.

We had no choice but to remove the water by hand.

I left my family behind, not knowing what would happen next, and went down to the bottom of the ship. We began emptying water using buckets , passing them hand to hand, throwing the water back into the ocean. It was exhausting. We were fighting to stay alive.

Our food was gone. Drinking water was nearly finished. We were lost at sea.

At that moment, I saw something that still hurts me. Many young men who were strong enough to help did nothing. Some were sick from the sea—understandable. The elderly could not help—also understandable. But many young people simply sat and waited.

Only about 20 to 30 of us worked continuously to keep the ship from sinking. I begged others to stand up and help, but most refused.

That night, the storm began.

The wooden ship rose and fell violently between massive waves. Every time we dropped, I felt we were only feet away from flipping over completely. Death was so close, yet it did not come.

Some people lost all hope—of reaching Australia, or even surviving. The darkness, rain, wind, broken ship, and isolation made the second night unbearable.

Still, many of us refused to give up. Even if death was waiting, we would not sit and watch it come. We continued emptying water all night until the third day arrived.

The third day was the same—water, sky, and exhaustion. No land. No help. As night approached again, we saw something far away. We didn't know if it was a ship or an island. Some people screamed. Some raised their hands. Some used lights.

Slowly, it came closer.

It was a large fishing ship—at least five times bigger than ours—with around 50 crew members. When we approached, the captain's son jumped into the ocean and swam bravely toward them. After they pulled him aboard, he explained everything.

The fishing ship was Indonesian. When they understood our situation, they decided to help.

They first tried to come alongside us, but the storm made it too dangerous—their ship could destroy ours. Then they tried sending a small boat, but the waves were too strong. They tried towing us with a rope, but the rope tore through our fragile wooden ship.

Finally, they told us to follow them slowly until morning.

We followed them through the night. By morning, the storm had passed. The sea became calm.

They sent the small boat again. This time, it worked. Women, children, and elderly were transferred first. The boat went back and forth many times until every single person was rescued.

Then we watched our ship sink—slowly disappearing beneath the ocean.

If that fishing ship had not found us, we would have died. I would not be writing this for you to read.

This taught me a lesson I will never forget:

If it is not your time to die, you will not die.

Not in war.

Not in the ocean.

Not anywhere.

Our lives end only when our purpose is complete. Every human life has a reason. Without knowing that reason, we live—and die—without ever understanding why we were born.

When we were inside that small wooden ship carrying more than one hundred people, we were seeing death with our own eyes. At any moment, we could have died while trying to survive. During those moments, I felt deep pain and guilt, because I was the one who decided to cross the ocean. If something had happened to my family and I was unable to help them, it would have been because of my decision. Yes, I was responsible for providing a future for my family, but not by risking their lives.

At that time, I no longer cared if I died. I only wished that my wife and my children would survive. Like many others on that ship, I did not know anything about boats or the ocean. We were all victims of lies and false promises.

After the large fishing ship rescued us, they treated us with kindness and humanity. They gave us food and water, and their captain contacted the Indonesian Navy to arrange where to deliver us. One day later, we arrived at the port, where navy ships, police, and journalists were waiting. We were happy to be alive, but we had no idea what would happen next.

After a few hours, we were taken by buses to a hotel because there was no place ready for us yet. Forty-eight hours later, we were transferred to prison.

From death to prison.

Families were separated from single men. From that moment, I never saw my friend who came with us again. The four families on the ship, including mine, were placed in separate cells close to each other. Each cell had nothing except a toilet with no door and a bare floor. No beds. No privacy. Imagine being imprisoned with your wife and two small children.

Every day in prison was painful, but the worst part was watching my family suffer while I could do nothing to protect them.

After two to three weeks, we learned that there was a way out. Our release depended on money. The prison governor demanded payment to pass our case to Australian immigration officials in Indonesia. We had no choice. All four families agreed, because prison with women and children was unbearable.

The cost was $500 per person. That money was almost everything I had left, but I paid without hesitation. Forty-five days later, Australian immigration helped secure our release. Without that payment, we could have stayed in prison for years.

After our release, we were taken back near the area where we had lived before. Australian immigration provided us with housing and monthly financial support to survive. We were safe, but our status was still uncertain. We waited again.

After one year, our case was reviewed by the Australian government. Then we waited two more years for the final decision. After nearly seven years since leaving our hometown, we finally received confirmation that we were accepted. The process was long, but our patience was rewarded.

Before continuing to the chapter about receiving our visas and tickets, there is one important story I must tell.

While living in Indonesia, I helped a man from my hometown whom I trusted. He arrived alone, carrying money entrusted to him by another friend. Instead of delivering it, he spent it. To protect my integrity and my friend's trust, my wife sold all her gold so I could repay the money.

Despite the betrayal, I continued helping him. He lived with us, ate our food, and I supported him. But when he began speaking badly about the same people who helped him, I ended it. I asked him to leave my home.

Later, he and his wife went to the police and accused us. The police came to our home, but after understanding the truth, they left. That experience taught me a painful lesson: not everyone who smiles is honest. Some people value money more than dignity, loyalty, or friendship.

This is not written to judge, but to warn.

Chapter 13

A Fragile Beginning

When we finally received our visas and flight tickets to Australia we felt happiness—relief that, at last, a country had accepted us as permanent residents. But that happiness was mixed with exhaustion. When we first left our hometown, we never imagined the journey would take nearly seven years of our lives, filled with loss, waiting, fear, and sacrifice. Even then, we did not know what was waiting for us in Australia. We only knew that we would have to start again from zero.

The greatest comfort in my heart was for my children. I did not want them to live the life we had lived—the fear, the instability, the constant struggle. My life, from childhood into adulthood, had never known true happiness, and I did not want that inheritance passed on to them.

I kept going and never gave up—not for myself, but for those who needed me. I sacrificed myself repeatedly to make others happy, without realizing that I first needed to take care of myself. I believed that if I stayed strong, everyone else would be fine. I did not understand then that neglecting myself would later cost me deeply. This is something I will explain more when the time comes.

The day finally arrived for us to leave Indonesia—legally, permanently, holding Australian visas. Some friends who had helped us when we first arrived in Indonesia had already reached Australia before us, as well as others who came later from Syria. And finally, it was our turn.

After nearly ten hours in the air, we arrived in Australia.

I believed this would be the place where life would finally become stable. Australia was a good country—but it did not bring peace to our family in the way I had hoped. At that time, I did not yet know that the hardest chapter of my personal life was still ahead.

Our two sons were enrolled in school immediately. My younger son was seven years old and entered first grade, and my older son entered third grade. They did not speak English at all, but they learned quickly—so quickly that, over time, they spoke English better than our own language.

The Australian government supported us when we arrived. They provided temporary accommodation for four weeks, helped us open bank accounts, and gave us access to medical care. After those four weeks, we had to find our own place to live. Eventually, we rented a two-bedroom apartment and moved out.

The financial support we received was helpful, but it was not enough to live comfortably or save. I began studying English through a government program and completed one term before enrolling in a higher-level college course called English for Further Study, which included speaking, reading, writing, listening, and basic computer skills.

Before finishing the course, I found work as a delivery driver for a privately owned family business. I left my studies and began working full-time, five days a week.

I worked hard. I left home early every morning while my family slept and returned late, depending on deliveries, traffic, and workload. Despite being in a safe country, our relationship did not improve. My wife and I slowly grew distant. We stayed together because our sons were still young and needed both parents present. That was my priority.

I devoted myself to my children. I was not only their father—I was their friend. Everything I lacked in my own childhood, I tried to give them: love, safety, play, encouragement. I took them to parks, enrolled them in football, bought them what I could afford, and showed them affection openly. In doing so, I forgot myself.

I avoided confronting the problems in my marriage and focused instead on making my sons happy. I had lived a life without understanding happiness, and I refused to let them inherit that pain. I love them deeply to this day, and they still love and respect me.

The divorce that came later broke me. After nearly twenty years of marriage, I never expected it to end. I know I made many mistakes—especially financial ones—that cost us stability. I did not lose millions, but I lost enough that, had I been wiser, our financial life could have been better.

Still, I was kind. I was respectful. I cared deeply for my wife and did everything I could for her. But kindness alone was not enough. I came to understand that many women need security—especially financial security—and when that weakens or does not improve, relationships begin to collapse.

Chapter 14

The Work, the Game, and the Breaking Point

After a few months of work, I noticed that the boss—who had become a friend—played football regularly with his younger brother. One day I told him that I used to play football when I was younger, though never professionally and never in a proper team with a coach. He smiled and said, "Come train with us. We need players for next season."

He was both the coach and a player, and the team was mixed in age—young men and older ones playing together.

I accepted and started training twice a week. He quickly saw that I was good: fast, committed, and playing with heart. I was in my forties then, very fit, no extra weight at all. Football was something I loved deeply, and whenever I played, I played the same way I did as a kid—with freedom, hunger, and joy.

When the season started, I played mostly as a left winger, sometimes in midfield when needed. My role was simple but demanding: attack when we had the ball, track back and defend when we didn't. I played every game, running more than most of my teammates. Slowly, we started winning. We climbed the ladder week by week.

Some teams were very strong. One team in particular was much younger than us and ran nonstop—they were our main competitors. We played them twice during the season. In the end, we finished first and won the league.

Then came the finals. The top four teams played again to decide the champion. We won our semifinal, the second-ranked team won theirs, and we met in the final. It was a hard, physical match. Both teams fought until the end. But we won.

That season, we won both the league and the championship—something the club had never achieved before. It was the first time they won both trophies together.

At work, life continued as usual—until the first injury.

One day in the warehouse, I was standing on the second step of a ladder, holding a heavy box with both hands while carrying my full weight on my legs. As I twisted to pass the box to a colleague, my back suddenly twisted badly. The pain was unbearable. I couldn't continue. I climbed down and lay on the warehouse floor. Even breathing hurts.

They called an ambulance and took me to the hospital. I was off work for two to three weeks, doing physiotherapy until I felt slightly better, then I returned.

A few months later, it happened again—this time during deliveries. I had loaded around 100 kilograms or more onto a two-wheel trolley. When there was no space left, I squatted, pulled the trolley upright, and heard a crack in my lower spine. A sharp, deep pain followed.

I didn't stop. I finished all my deliveries, then called my boss and told him what had happened. The next day, after an MRI, doctors confirmed a lower spine injury. A specialist recommended cortisone injections. I took one, then another, then another. I did physiotherapy, chiropractic treatment, acupuncture, hydrotherapy—nothing helped. The third injury came in the warehouse again. This time, I lifted only a five-kilogram box from the floor to place it in the van, and the same pain returned—sharp, familiar, devastating.

After repeating the same cycle—time off, treatment, return to work—I finally had to face reality. The specialist told me surgery was now my choice. Nothing else had worked.

By then, I had already been working there for four and a half years. Nothing in my life had changed. I was working hard every day, getting older, just paying rent and living expenses, carrying responsibilities—but going nowhere.

I asked myself: Why did I come here? Was this the better life I was searching for?

I decided to quit. Instead of giving four weeks' notice, I gave three months so they could find a replacement. I trained the new worker and passed on everything I had learned. When I finally left, it was the longest job I had ever stayed in—but I left injured.

The boss, who had been my friend, tried hard to convince me to stay. I refused. I told him this wasn't good for me or for the company. I was constantly injured, always off work, always returning just to repeat the same cycle. That wasn't who I was.

Chapter 15

Wounds, Distance, and the Cost of Loyalty

When I left, the friendship ended too. That's when I learned a painful truth: friendships at work often exist only while you are useful. Once you leave, they disappear.

After my surgery, while lying in the hospital bed on the second day, I took a photo of myself and sent it to him. His reply was short, cold, and empty. Nothing more. That moment stayed with me. I understood then that I had to start taking care of myself—because when you have no family beside you, life becomes even harder.

Because I was covered by insurance, I received 80% of my salary for five years since I couldn't return to the same job. Later, they paid me a lump sum—but I was cheated, simply because I didn't understand how the system worked.

When the five years ended, the payments stopped immediately. I had no choice but to return to government support.

By then, I was broken physically—and my relationship was slowly breaking too. I tried everything I could to fix our life. I was scammed several times while trying to make money. Each failure disappointed my wife more. Disrespect slowly replaced patience between us.

Later, I sent her overseas to visit her family and to look for her daughter—whom she hadn't heard from for many years. She had given her daughter back to the father before we left our hometown, and that pain never left her. It was one of the deepest wounds in our life together.

Another wound was the tension between her and my family, especially my sisters and my mother. Because of her, and to keep my promise, I didn't speak to my three sisters for sixteen years.

One and a half years before we planned to travel as a family, my second-oldest brother passed away. His death broke me before I ever had the chance to see him again.

That loss pushed me to reconnect with my sisters. One day, my younger brother sent me a message from one of them—she was crying and asking to see me after our brother's death. Until then, I didn't even know how they were living. I didn't know their children, and their children didn't know me.

I decided to end the distance.

Before doing so, I spoke to my wife. I told her that I needed to talk to my sisters again, even if she didn't like it. I reminded her that I knew my family before I knew her, and that despite everything, I had always stood by her and never abandoned her.

I had booked a ticket for her four months in advance, planning for us and our sons to visit my family. She found her daughter during that trip, spent time with her, and became happy.

I also booked tickets for the three of us to visit my family, planning that she would return with us to Australia afterward. I reserved a three-day stay in Dubai, hoping we could enjoy some privacy, visit another country, and let my sons have some fun.

But nothing went as planned. Everything began to unravel within the first four or five days of visiting my family.

The first big mistake—and the one that caused everything to collapse—was when I got scammed out of more than $100,000. Half of that money was hers, and it came from a bank loan we had both taken. We had invested it together in a company. I accepted that it was my mistake to lose the money in a fake company. It wasn't intentional, only a result of lack of information. Many others had been scammed too, losing even more than we did. I knew that, but it didn't change the loss.

While we were visiting my family, she insisted that she wanted her money back. At that moment, I felt confused and shattered. Were we partners in life, or partners only in money? Could she really forget all the ups and downs we had survived together? We had shared so many years, raised our sons, and faced challenges that would have broken many couples. Now, in this moment, it felt like all of that meant nothing.

Our sons, already adults by now, were witnessing this. The trip, which was meant to be a joyful reunion with family, was turning into a nightmare. My plan had been clear: one week with my family, three days in Dubai, and then two weeks visiting the Sultanate of Oman, where one of my nephews lives. But everything fell apart.

When my family left after one week, and our flight to Dubai was only a few hours later, she asked me for a divorce. The trip was ruined, my sons were already upset by everything they had experienced, and this was supposed to be their first time visiting my family—a family that had welcomed them with love, respect, and care.

From her family, only her mother came to visit us. My family had covered her travel and stayed out of their own pockets; she didn't contribute a single cent.

Despite all of this, when I confronted her about the divorce, she confirmed: "Yes, we decided. When we return to Australia, I will follow through with the divorce process."

And with that, we left for Dubai, the weight of the trip's collapse heavy on all of us.

We had been through so much together. Throughout our life, I always respected her—first as a woman, then as my partner, and as the mother of my two sons. I gave her freedom, dignity, and space. Even during this last year, when she said many painful things that broke my heart, I continued to stand by her. I did so because of a promise I made before our marriage: that I would respect her, care for her, and never let her down. But sometimes, life does not go the way we hope.

When I saw her disrespect me in front of my family after all those years, something inside me finally broke. At that moment, it felt as though she had replaced me with money and forgotten everything we had shared—the struggles, the sacrifices, the years we survived together from the very beginning. That was when I told myself: enough. It was time for each of us to go our own way.

We flew to Dubai, where my nephew was waiting for us with his wife. We went to the hotel. I had already booked two rooms—one for my sons and one for her and me. But there was nothing left between us that could allow us to stay in the same room. I asked my younger son to sleep with her, while I stayed with my older son. Later, I understood that he didn't want to stay with her, but because he respected me, he accepted it.

I tried to stay calm and composed during the trip. My only goal was to keep my promise to my sons and make them happy, at least for a short time. But my younger son was deeply upset. If he had been able to choose, he would have left the trip early and gone back home.

We visited several places in Dubai together—the Burj Khalifa, the Museum of the Future, and the beach. I had also booked a one-day Sahara desert tour as part of the three-day stay. She refused to come with us, just as she distanced herself everywhere we went, always leaving space between us, walking alone or sometimes with my nephew's wife. Even my nephew began to notice what was happening. It was painful to witness the collapse of a trip we had planned for years.

My younger son also didn't want to go to the desert because of how upset he was. But in the end, I convinced him to come with us. That day, it was just me and my two sons. She stayed at the hotel with my nephew and his wife, and they went out together during the day.

We left the hotel in the morning and returned late at night after the tour ended. Despite everything, that day became something special. We rode motorcycles on the sand, rode camels, and joined the other desert activities. For a few hours, it was just a father and his sons, sharing laughter and presence.

Later that night, my younger son thanked me for taking him and not leaving him behind at the hotel. Seeing both my sons enjoy themselves—even for one day—brought me peace.

After the three days in Dubai ended, we continued our journey to the Sultanate of Oman, to my nephew's home.

We stayed in Oman for two weeks. During the first week, one of my brothers visited us with his family, and later he came back again and stayed with us for some time. We spent time together, and on the surface everything looked fine—but not from the heart. Not from the inside. We were showing others that we were happy, but the truth was very different.

We went fishing twice. One day we rented a farm with a swimming pool and a furnished house and spent the day there.

Most of the remaining days were filled with shopping, mainly for the women. Another nephew came with his mother, and my brother also brought my other brother's wife and her daughter. At one point, there were around thirteen people staying together. Slowly, one family after another left, until we were the last ones to return to Australia.

In reality, my sons and I were not happy at all. We wanted the trip to end quickly and to go back home. Even while we were in Oman, and before that in the UAE, she continued to ask me for money—and I gave it to her. Yet she barely spoke to me.

My brother noticed that we were not talking and asked me about it. He was confused, because she was very polite and respectful with my family, and everyone treated her with respect as well. When he asked me why we were divorcing, I told him the truth—that it was her decision, not mine. Of course, my family did not know what was really happening between us. From the outside, they believed we were one of the happiest couples. But outside is often very different from inside—not only in relationships, but in life itself.

A rose has beauty, color, and a beautiful scent, yet it also has thorns. Life is the same. People are the same. We cannot judge someone by what we see on the surface, and we are not even entitled to judge others without knowing their inner world and their past.

When we returned home, I started sleeping on the living room floor and began looking for another place to live. I could no longer stay in that house—especially after she turned my older son against me. He was the one I loved deeply from the moment he was born. He changed completely, choosing a path that created emotional and religious boundaries between us. He began seeing life from only one direction, one angle.

At that moment, I realized that the place I once called my family was no longer my family. I had already lost it. My younger son was much closer to me during that period. He could see the truth, but he was powerless to change anything. When he realized that I was looking for a place to move out, he became very sad. He didn't want me to leave—but everything between us as a family was already over.

After nearly two months of searching, I found a shared house with a couple who wanted to rent out one of their rooms. I inspected the place, we talked, and we agreed that I would move in the next day.

When I went back home, I told them simply:

"I'm moving out tomorrow morning."

The only person who showed sadness and pain was my younger son.

I was shocked by how my life had turned out. I was deeply sad and hurt—especially seeing how we were breaking apart.

The next morning, only my younger son was home when I left. We both tried hard not to cry in front of each other. Leaving him was one of the hardest moments of my life, but I had no other choice.

I told him to stay strong, that I would always stay connected to him, and that I would never leave him emotionally—no matter where I lived.

The place I moved to was only ten minutes away by car. Yet despite the short distance, the first two weeks were unbearable. I felt as if someone was slowly killing me. I couldn't breathe properly. For twenty years, I had lived with my family, seen my sons every day, hugged them, kissed them morning and night. Suddenly, I was alone.

Not only alone—but lonely.

I no longer felt their presence, their energy, or their warmth. And this is where my next journey began—a journey that was extremely hard and far from easy to get used to.

Chapter 16

Learning to Live Again

I began living with that couple, who were kind and welcoming from the beginning. The more they got to know me, the more they liked me—and I felt the same toward them. I respected them deeply, respected their privacy, and felt grateful that I had found a place like this. Still, it took me a long time to adjust to this new life. After twenty years of marriage, learning how to live as a single man was not easy at all.

If you are reading my story and you have lived through something similar, you will understand this feeling better than anyone else. You won't just read my words—you will feel them.

Because of my physical condition, I was unable to work. After my insurance payments stopped, I began receiving government support. The amount was just enough to survive: to pay rent in a shared house, cover basic living expenses, and sometimes try to save—although in reality, there was nothing to save.

With such limited income, it was impossible for me to rent a place on my own, even a small one-bedroom apartment. In Western countries—such as Europe, the USA, Australia, Canada, and others—renting is not simple. You must prove that you have a strong, stable income. It is not enough to want a place; the landlord and real estate agent must accept you.

For example, if the rent for a one-bedroom apartment is $500 per week, and your income is only $600–800 per week, you will most likely be rejected. They usually expect you to earn at least $1,000 per week or more. If another applicant earns $1,200 per week, they will be chosen instead. This is the reality. That is why I rented one room in a shared house—to survive.

Living there brought both positive and negative experiences, and I want to explain them honestly so you understand how this period affected me.

I will begin with the positive.

I was living with two kind, respectful, honest, quiet, and loving people who had been together for more than thirty years. They rented me one bedroom in their own home. Even though I was paying rent, I was truly grateful—it is not easy to find people like them.

They were clean, organized, and made me feel comfortable. Slowly, I began to feel as if I was living in my own home again. We shared the kitchen, and I shared the bathroom with the man of the house, who later became a close friend. He was gentle, wise, respectful, and very calm. I learned many things from him. His wife was also a kind and intelligent woman. She treated me with respect, and I treated her like a sister or a family member.

The more time I spent with them, the less I wanted to go anywhere else—and they felt the same. After only a few months, during a simple conversation, the woman said something that stayed with me deeply. She told me that even if they ever decided to sell their house and move elsewhere, they would take me with them.

Tears filled my eyes, but I held them back. I thought to myself: These people have known me for only a few months, yet they treat me with such kindness. I lived with someone for more than twenty years—look how that ended.

I do not complain about what happened in my life, and I do not point fingers. I accept my own mistakes. What hurt me most was not that mistakes were made, but that the other person never accepted their share of responsibility. No relationship fails because of one person alone. Yet I was always the one who apologized just to end arguments and keep peace.

I am writing this so you understand something important: no one is perfect. We all make mistakes. But when there is real love, respect, and understanding, mistakes can be acknowledged and forgiven. When these things are missing, sometimes it is better for a relationship to end sooner rather than later. That is what happened in my life.

I am not encouraging anyone to end their relationship. I am sharing my experience so that if you find yourself in a similar situation, you may try to fix it before it becomes worse—before it costs you years of your life.

Life does not reward people simply for being kind, nice, or good-hearted. Life rewards patience, wisdom, effort, emotional intelligence, and the ability to respond thoughtfully to problems. I learned this through my own mistakes. I had no guide, no mentor—no one to teach me these lessons before I paid their price.

All of us live this life for the first time. We are getting married for the first time. We learn by falling. If we knew everything in advance, no one would ever make mistakes. Some people make one mistake and never repeat it. Others, like me, make many—under different circumstances—until they finally understand that these mistakes cost more than money. They cost time. They cost life itself.

Let me go back a little and speak about family—after I visited mine for the first time in sixteen years. I did not visit my hometown, but another country nearby, to avoid any danger or legal consequences. I did not want to risk my life or my sons' lives after everything we had sacrificed.

Family is something you will never find a replacement for in this life. These are the people who teach you what father, mother, brother, and sister mean. They are not only family—they are your first and truest friends.

Some people grow up without parents, without siblings, without family support. Others, like me, grow up in large families and truly understand what family means. Even if someone does not experience it early, they may learn it later by building their own family and teaching their children respect, care, and love.

When I left my country with my wife and two young sons, my father was still strong at seventy-seven years old. He was forty-five years older than me. I was his eighth child—after five older brothers and two older sisters—and I also had three younger siblings: one brother and two sisters.

While I was still in Syria, I received the news that my father had gone blind. A surgery meant to improve his sight had failed, leaving him completely blind. I cried deeply over this. I used to call my family occasionally and speak with my parents and siblings. As my father grew older, he often asked me for forgiveness during our phone calls. That hurt me deeply. I never expected such words from my father.

He worked day and night to raise eleven children. He did everything he could with the knowledge and strength he had.

There was nothing for me to forgive. If anything, I felt I should be the one asking forgiveness.

Later, my second younger sister—who cared for both my parents and then my mother alone—told me something that brought me peace. She said my parents were always proud of me and never spoke badly about me. Hearing that meant more to me than words can express.

When I finally saw my family after sixteen years, everything had changed. Both my parents were in wheelchairs. My father was not only blind—he was deaf and suffering from Alzheimer's. He could not recognize or remember anyone. My brothers were caring for him with great dignity: feeding him, washing him, and protecting him.

He did not see me. He did not hear me. He may not have remembered me. But I am certain he felt me—with his heart.

From childhood, we were taught to respect our elders, especially our parents. That lesson never left me.

Chapter 17

Respect, Reunion, and Loss

After many years of distance, silence, and unanswered questions, something inside me shifted. Life had already taken so much from me — war, prison, an ocean crossing, refugee camps, marriage breakdown — and yet, the greatest absence in my heart was not wounds inflicted by the world, but the absence of my own family's presence.

My second-oldest brother had passed away. No warnings. No chance to see him again. When I received the news, a heavy emptiness settled inside me — deeper than anything I had felt before. I cried knowing he had left without a final word, a final hug, a final chance to say goodbye.

At that moment, I knew something had to change. The distance between me and my sisters — sixteen years of silence — suddenly felt unbearable. I thought about our parents. I thought about the years lost, the unanswered laughter, the unshared grief. And I decided it was time.

I spoke to my wife about it. I told her I needed to visit my sisters, to reconnect, to finally face the family I had left behind so long ago. She was quiet at first — unsure, maybe uncomfortable with the idea of reopening old wounds. But I reminded her: *This family is a part of me that I never fully left. They raised me, shaped me, and lived through the same hardships I lived through. I needed to see them — not for me alone, but for the boy I once was.*

I booked the tickets months in advance. My plan was simple: visit my siblings, heal old hurts, and then move forward stronger than before.

When the day arrived, my heart was thick with emotion. I wasn't sure what I expected — joy, fear, guilt, relief — maybe all of them mixed together. When we finally saw each other, time did not slow. It did not soften. It simply became real. We wept. We held hands. We spoke of lost years as if the years themselves stood between us.

But nothing compared to seeing my parents again.

They had aged — decades older than the last time I saw them. Their faces carried time like a story I had missed reading. My father, once strong and steady, now sat in a wheelchair, blind, deaf, and tangled in the fog of Alzheimer's. He did not see me — not with his eyes, not with his ears — but I knew he felt me.

I spoke to him softly, placing my hand over his. I said nothing long, nothing loud, just simple words carried from the depths of memory:

Your son is here.

I have come back.

His lips moved. Not in words — not clearly — but there was recognition in the tremor, in the warmth of his hand around mine. Even when his mind could no longer hold memories, something in his heart remembered.

My mother leaned forward. Her eyes, though clouded with age, still carried tenderness. She reached for me — not with urgency — but with a quiet knowing that surpassed memory. I cried again, not out of sorrow, but because certain truths return no matter how far you travel: family is the beginning and the end of who we are.

My sisters hugged me. We sat close to each other and shared stories of what was lost, of time wasted, of pain endured. Each of them told me I was forgiven, that distance had not broken love. One of my sisters, through tears, said something I will never forget:

"Your family never stopped loving you. We only waited for you to come home in your heart."

That night, we ate, we talked, we cried, we remembered. And the next day, when I looked into my parents' faces — no longer youthful, no longer strong — I understood something deeper:

When you leave home, you may lose memories.
When you return, you may find that love was waiting, not lost.

But life is fragile.

One year later, I received news that pierced my heart deeply. My father had passed away in his sleep—quietly and without struggle. About three months later, my mother followed him. Losing them both within such a short time was something I never imagined I would face.

Because of the safety risks and the legal situation surrounding the country I had left, I could not return for their funerals. If I had gone back, I might have been arrested and imprisoned.

This was a pain I had to carry silently—the pain of not being able to say goodbye in person.

For this reason, I met them in a different country after sixteen years, without risking my life or my sons' lives. That meeting became the last time I saw them, and I hold that memory with gratitude.

I was no longer the boy who left with a dream of freedom.
 I was no longer the man who ran from pain.
 I was a son — a brother — a man who finally reunited with his family after many years.

The loss still pained me, but it was a different kind of pain — the kind that shows love was real, not temporary. The kind that shows respect was present all along, even when life's distance taught us silence instead of words.

And in that silence, I learned something essential:

Even if eyes cannot see, a heart can still feel.
 Even if memories fade, love remembers.

That is what they taught me.

Chapter 18

The Divorce and Leaving My Home

Before I left the house where we had lived together for nearly twenty years, I told my wife something very important.

I said to her that even if we were getting divorced, she could always ask me for help if she needed anything. I told her that we were not enemies. We had two sons together, and they needed both of us in their lives.

I also understood that she was living abroad just like me. None of her family members were close to her except our two sons and me. Even though we were separating because she no longer wanted the marriage, I still felt responsible for her well-being as the mother of my children.

But I could clearly see that she did not want me anymore, and honestly, I still couldn't believe what I was experiencing.

During our years of marriage, there were moments when she told me that she had never truly loved me and that she had married me mainly because she wanted to leave her parents' house and have more freedom in her life with her daughter from her first marriage.

Usually she said these things when she was upset and thinking about the past. During those moments she blamed me for many things and made me feel like I was the only one who had made mistakes.

I tried to be patient and stay calm, but those words hurt me deeply. At the same time, there were other moments when she told me that she loved me very much, and those moments made me forget the painful things she had said before.

This pattern happened many times over the years, and eventually I became used to it.

I often tried to look at our relationship from different perspectives. Sometimes I believed we were truly in love. Other times it felt like we were simply living together because of circumstances. But no matter what, I stayed with my family as long as I could because I did not want our family to fall apart, especially for the sake of our two sons.

Before I left the house and moved into a shared accommodation, she had already found a job and started working. My older son was also working in a company at that time.

However, after I left the house, he left his job. I learned this later from my younger son because my older son had stopped speaking to me for several months.

Before I left the house, we also received unexpected news from the real estate agent. The owner of the house wanted to move back in, which meant we had to leave the property.

By that time, I had already decided to leave because I felt there was no place for me in that home anymore.

I packed my personal belongings and left everything else for them. I left the rental bond for them so they could use it when renting their next home. All the furniture and household items stayed with them as well.

Knowing they had everything they needed gave me some peace, even though leaving was very painful.

But the hardest part was not just my separation from my wife. My older son had also turned against me and stopped speaking to me while I was still living with them.

This was not the first time he had stopped talking to me. It had happened once before for nearly six months. Later, when he realized he had been wrong, he came back to me and apologized. I forgave him and never showed him how hurt I had been.

This time, however, the situation was different.

The main reason behind his change was religion. As he became more deeply involved in religious teachings, he began to see life only from that perspective. I tried many times to speak with him and explain different points of view, but he believed he was right and that I was wrong.

My son is a good person, and he still is. But at that time he was young and strongly influenced by his new understanding of religion.

I personally respect people from every religion, every culture, every background, and every race. For me, the most important thing is humanity. I try to respect every person simply because they are human beings.

Religion can teach many beautiful values. Unfortunately, some people misuse religion for their own beliefs, control, or benefit. But I do not want to go deeply into that subject in this book.

Everyone has the right to believe, think, and live freely.

I hope that one day all human beings can live in peace regardless of religion, language, culture, country, or skin color. In the end, we are all human beings. From the outside we may look different, but inside we all share the same human heart and soul.

Chapter 19

After I Left

When I left the house, I believe my wife did not expect that I would actually go. But by that time things had reached a point where I had no other choice.

After I moved out, they started looking for another house to rent. Even though we were separated, I still tried to help them find a place. I searched for houses at real estate agencies and online, but I only did this quietly with my younger son without telling her.

We found several possible houses, and I even attended some inspections with my younger son. But she did not accept those options.

Eventually, I found a house available very close to where I was living in my shared accommodation. I couldn't attend the inspection myself, but I told my younger son about it and said that the rent might suit their budget.

They inspected the house, applied for it, and were accepted. The house was only a few minutes' walk from where I was living, but neither my wife nor my older son knew where I was staying until later.

When they moved into the new house, she did not ask for my help. I tried to organize a truck to help them move their furniture, but she told my younger son to simply take the phone number from me and give it to her.

By that time she had stopped speaking to me completely.

One day I went to the house while she was at work. My younger son was there alone, and I helped pack and dismantle the king-size bed and some other furniture to make the move easier for them. It was the first time they were moving house without me, so I wanted to help.

Later, when she found out I had been there, she became very angry with my younger son and said that I was not allowed to come to the house again.

After that, she still needed help with some plumbing fixtures in the bathroom that I had originally installed. She asked my younger son to call me.

I was confused. On one hand she did not want me in the house, but on the other hand she still needed my help.

I told my son to let me know when she was not at home, and I would come to remove the fixtures.

It had already been about two months since I left the house. When I came to help, my older son was there, but he stayed in his room and never came out to see me.

I finished the job and left.

Later I told my son to let me know when they moved into the new house so I could reinstall the same fixtures there. However, she said she did not want me to enter the new house.

Once again, I was confused. In the end, I still helped them reinstall everything when she was not there.

Signing the Divorce

During that time I had already started the divorce process.

I spoke to a lawyer and offered to pay all the legal costs so that the process could be simple and peaceful for both of us. The lawyer explained that we would not need to attend court. We only needed to sign the documents, have them witnessed by a Justice of the Peace (JP), and send them back.

The lawyer would handle the rest and represent us in court.

She agreed.

After some time, the documents arrived. We arranged a date and time to meet at the JP office to sign them.

I arrived before her and waited for my turn.

When she arrived, she did not look at me or say hello.

It was a strange and painful moment. After spending so many years together—sharing our lives, our home, and our children—we were now standing there like strangers.

The JP checked our identification, asked a few questions, and then we both signed the divorce documents.

After that, we simply left without saying a word to each other.

Even today, I want to pause here and say something important.

I thank her from my heart for the years we shared together. She stood beside me during many good and difficult times. She supported me, cared for me, and worked very hard for our family.

She was the mother of my two sons.

She had also suffered greatly in her life before meeting me, including difficulties from her first marriage. For those reasons I always tried to respect her, love her, and make her happy as much as I could.

But I was not perfect. I made mistakes, especially financially. I often tried to improve our situation, but sometimes my decisions led to losses instead of success.

Even so, I still respect her as a human being.

A few months later the divorce was finalized, and we each received the official court documents from the lawyer.

Chapter 20

My Sons

I lived with my sons from the day they were born until my youngest was seventeen years old. That was when I left home after the separation and later the divorce.

My sons were everything to me then, and they still are today, even though they are now adults in their early twenties.

I never imagined that something like this would happen in my life. Losing the life we built together broke me deeply and caused a pain that is hard to describe.

I shared so many memories with my sons — both in the good days and in the difficult ones. I was not only their father; I was also their friend.

One thing I always tried to give them was the love that I did not fully experience when I was growing up. I am not blaming my father for that. His life was different. I had two children, but he had eleven. Every person's life is different. But when I say that I showed my sons love, I truly mean it — and they know it and feel it.

What I did for the older one, I did for the younger one as well. Even something as simple as a kiss, I never wanted one to feel less loved than the other. When they were children, I loved them deeply, and that love has never changed.

When you live with your children every day, seeing them in the morning and at night, spending time together during the day, taking them to sports, registering them in teams, picking them up from school, waiting for them to finish their training, or even going to school when they had problems or fights with other kids — all of these moments become part of your life.

These are things that no one did for me when I was a child, but I wanted my sons to experience them.

I was always there for them. And even today, if they need me at any time, I will still be there.

But the pain of not living with them anymore is something that remains inside me. It reminds me of what happened in our lives. I always imagined that we would live together as a family until they grew up, got married, and started their own families.

I never imagined that my life with them would end because of divorce.

I did many things for my sons and always tried to teach them to respect others and be good people. My sons were my life. But after the divorce and the pain that followed, everything I had built as a family suddenly disappeared.

It felt as if my life had returned to the beginning — as if I had never been married and never had a family.

But no matter what happens in life, one truth will never change: I am their father, and they are my sons.

Wherever I go, they are always in my heart, even if that heart is sometimes broken.

Losing my family through divorce was one of the hardest experiences of my life. In some ways, it felt even worse than death, because everyone was still alive, but the life we had together was gone. The last time we truly enjoyed time together was when we traveled to Dubai. Even though it was a short trip,

We had moments of happiness together before everything collapsed.

After that, I continued to live, but in reality I was only alive — I was not truly living.

I know that the situation was not easy for my sons either. It was difficult for their mother as well. I never wanted our life to end this way.

Even now, while writing this book, I sometimes wish we could still live together — not as a broken family, but simply as a father and his two sons sharing life under the same roof.

Instead, sometimes I see my sons in the street, or once a week, or sometimes once a month.

Writing about my sons and my relationship with them could fill an entire book by itself. There are so many memories, stories, and emotions that cannot all fit into these pages.

I hope that no one experiences the same pain that I went through. Of course, many people face divorce and different struggles in life. Every person has their own story and their own challenges.

I am not saying that my pain is greater than anyone else's.

What I mean is this: whatever happens in your life, stay strong. Try to control your mind, and do not let your mind control you and destroy you from inside.

Sometimes I think that if another person had experienced everything I went through, they might have become lost in alcohol, anger, or even given up on life completely.

But one thing about me is that I never gave up.

Even when I was broken inside, I stayed strong on the outside.

I stayed strong first for myself, and then for my sons and the other people in my life who might one day need my help.

That is what kept me moving forward through so much pain — along with the hope, the dreams, and the goals I still have for my life. Whether I achieve those dreams or not is not the most important thing.

The most important thing is that I never gave up trying.

Even if it is the last day of my life, I will continue trying.

Chapter 21

My Son Comes Back / Moving Forward

For nearly a year after the divorce, I could only see my younger son. My older son had blocked my number, cutting off all contact. Then, unexpectedly, he called.

Before that day, I had sent him a birthday message, even though he had deleted my contact entirely. When he finally reached out, asking if he could visit, my heart felt a mix of relief, joy, and hope. His voice was calm, respectful, and kind. I hugged him, kissed him, and accepted his apology. I told him to forget the past and embrace forgiveness.

This reunion reminded me that the past should guide us, not trap us. My ex-wife and I were struggling, my sons were adjusting to new realities, and life had changed for all of us.

Seeing my sons live their lives outside of my home was painful. I watched them in the streets, day and night, in winter and summer, unable to enter the house where they lived. My older son's religious beliefs and my ex-wife's decisions made it impossible. I wanted to live nearby, to be present as a father, but the circumstances would not allow it.

I suggested a compromise: if their mother agreed, I could live with them and contribute to the rent, bills, cooking, and daily life instead of paying rent to strangers in a shared house. My intention was simply to support them and remain close without creating problems in their home. My younger son understood, but my older son hesitated. After discussion with their mother, the plan fell through. It was a painful realization: life could not go back to the way it was.

I accepted reality. I could survive anywhere, rebuild my life, and support my sons in other ways. I would never force my presence at the expense of their mother's comfort. I promised myself: if they ever needed me, I would always be there.

Slowly, over time, my older son began seeing me more regularly. Respect, patience, and love rebuilt our bond. My younger son remained in touch, understanding more than people thought. I guided them, encouraged their interests, and reminded them to pursue their goals, whether in football or life.

During this period, I also tried to rebuild financially. Over four years, I invested in cryptocurrency and NFTs, hoping to recover what we had lost earlier. I patiently waited, watching my investments grow to around $150,000. But one night, everything vanished. I had been scammed online. All my efforts, savings, and hope evaporated in an instant.

That loss crushed me. Everything I had worked for—my family, my stability, my dreams—felt as though it had collapsed. I asked myself a question I had never faced so starkly: What now? How could I survive, especially with my physical condition limiting my work?

Before continuing my story, I must return to an important trip I once made to Thailand—one that changed my perspective and played a role in how I chose to move forward in life.

Chapter22

Thailand

After my divorce, I spent a few months living alone in shared accommodation. It was a quiet place, but inside me there was a lot of noise.

Before all of this, my life had been full of people. First there was my big family — my parents, my brothers, my sisters, and all their children. Later there was my own small family — my wife and my two sons. For many years I was surrounded by people every day.

Then suddenly everything became quiet.

When we write about time in a book, it is easy to say "a few days," "a few weeks," or "a few months." But living those days in real life is very different. Every single day feels long when you are carrying pain inside you.

Each twenty-four hours can feel like a long journey between two emotions: happiness or sadness.

Loneliness is something I truly hope that you, as a reader, will never experience.

Being alone is very different from feeling lonely. Only those who have experienced both understand the difference.

After those months of loneliness, I began thinking about meeting another woman. Not necessarily to start a serious relationship, but maybe just to spend some time together, talk, and feel some human connection again.

I have been married for twenty years. During that time I never had to search for affection anywhere else. I also was never the type of person who visited places where many men go just to satisfy themselves.

I am not saying that those men are wrong. Everyone lives their life in their own way. I simply knew that it was not the kind of person I was.

I always believed in having one woman in my life, just like I had before. What I wanted was simple: someone I could love and someone who could love me. For me, that was enough.

After my younger son moved back to live with his mother, I decided to save some money and travel overseas for a while. I chose to visit an Asian country where living costs were not too expensive.

That country was Thailand.

Before deciding to travel there, I had a friend who had already visited Thailand many times. He even owned a small apartment there that he rented out. Because of his experience, he knew a lot about the country and often told me that I should go and visit.

When many people hear the name Thailand, they immediately think only about sex tourism. But the truth is different.

First, not everyone who goes there is looking for that.

Second, Thailand is much more than that image. The country has beautiful culture, amazing food, incredible places to visit, and very kind and friendly people.

There are also many respectable women there who would never even look at foreign men in that way.

Those types of places exist mainly in certain tourist areas. But the truth is that similar things exist everywhere in the world. Every country has them, even if people do not talk about it openly.

My friend had suggested many times that I should travel there with him. But I never liked the idea of going alone. I hoped that one day we could travel together so that I could benefit from his experience.

At that time my mind was still full of thoughts from the past. I was still emotionally affected by everything that had happened in my marriage.

I was fifty-fifty about going.

After speaking with my friend several times, he encouraged me again to travel and relax for a while. Finally, I decided to book a ticket. I planned to stay there for about three weeks.

My friend said that if his work allowed him, he might travel at the same time. I hoped that would happen so that I would not be completely alone during my first visit.

After booking my ticket and before I travel, I started searching for more information about the country.

During that time I also met a woman online who lived in Thailand. We met on a Thai dating website. After speaking for some time on the website, we exchanged contact details and continued talking through another social media application.

Soon we were talking every day.

We exchanged photos and messages. Eventually I asked if we could have a video call, because I believed that seeing each other face-to-face was important.

When we had our video call, she appeared exactly the same as in her photos. She looked attractive, and she seemed kind and respectful in conversation.

She had many of the qualities I was hoping to find in a woman.

Slowly I began to like her.

But at the same time, I tried several times to end the communication. Because of my personal situation, I did not want to give her false hope. However, each time I tried to step back, she became very emotional and asked me not to leave.

Eventually we continued talking until the date of my travel came closer.

We planned that we would meet when I arrived in Thailand.

But during our conversations before the trip, there were a few moments when I felt that she might not be telling me the full truth. Something inside my heart felt uncertain.

Each time I asked her about it, she denied it and insisted that she was telling the truth.

In the end I decided that the only way to know the truth was to see things with my own eyes.

A few days before my departure, my friend managed to book his ticket as well. He actually traveled two days before me, which made me feel more relaxed because I knew someone would be there when I arrived.

The day finally came.

When I arrived at the airport in Bangkok, my friend was waiting for me. For the first few days we stayed together in the city.

After three days, I left my friend and traveled to another city where the woman lived. The city was about four hours away from Bangkok.

She stayed in contact with me constantly while I was traveling, asking every few minutes where I was and when I would arrive. She told me that she would come to pick me up at the bus terminal.

When I arrived, she told me to wait for her at a specific place.

I waited there for about fifteen minutes. Then I noticed a woman arriving on a motorcycle, stopping exactly where I was supposed to be waiting.

She looked around, clearly searching for someone.

But from a distance I immediately realized something shocking.

She looked completely different from the woman I had seen in the photos and video calls.

It was not the same person.

At that moment I understood everything.

Later I learned that she had been using heavy filters to make herself appear younger and more attractive.

Even though I was shocked, I was not completely surprised. Something inside me had already warned me that this might happen.

I raised my hand to show her where I was standing.

She drove the motorcycle toward me, picked me up, and took me to a nearby hotel close to the bus terminal.

Inside I felt confused. I still could not believe what I was seeing.

She quickly realized that I was disappointed.

She asked me what I wanted to do next.

I told her honestly that things were not what I expected, but I did not want to hurt her feelings. I explained that we could remain friends, but that I would probably return to Bangkok soon.

Before traveling, I had brought a gift for her and also a small gift for her daughter, whom she had told me about. She was divorced and living with her daughter.

When I gave her the gifts, she seemed surprised. Maybe she did not expect that after what had happened I would still give them to her.

But I wanted to show her that even if she had not been honest with me, I would still behave honestly and respectfully.

I stayed in her city for two days. During that time she showed me around a few places and we ate together, but nothing more happened between us.

After two days I returned to Bangkok and joined my friend again.

For the rest of the trip we explored different places, tried new food, and visited new areas. I tried my best to enjoy the experience.

But the truth is that my mind was not ready for travel yet. I was not ready to start another relationship either.

I realized that I still needed time to find myself again.

The main lesson I learned from that experience was that online dating can be very different from meeting someone in real life.

When you meet someone face-to-face in your own city, you can understand them more easily. You can feel their personality and their honesty. But in the modern world, many things are changing — including the way people meet and start relationships.

Eventually my trip ended and I returned home to my shared accommodation.

Not long after that, the next major loss in my life happened.

That was the night I was scammed online and lost the investment I had spent four years building.

Once again, I felt broken.

But the only thing that kept me moving forward was hope. I had already experienced many losses in my life, and I knew that no one could rebuild my life for me except myself.

After losing everything that night, I decided to leave the shared accommodation and try a different lifestyle.

That experiment lasted only about six months.

After that, I returned to the same place again and moved back in with the kind couple who had rented me the room before.

This story — and what happened during that period of my life — is something I will explain later

Chapter 23

My Niece

I met my niece for the first time when she was around sixteen years old. Even though she had been born many years earlier, I had never had the chance to meet her because I had been away from my family for a long time. I finally met her when she was about sixteen years old, during the same visit when I reunited with the rest of my family after many years apart.

When we first started talking and getting to know each other, her father was still alive and I was still married. From the beginning, our conversations were long and meaningful. Whenever we spoke, it was rarely less than an hour. Many times we talked for two, three, or even four hours at a time.

Slowly, we began to understand each other better. We connected almost every day, without thinking about where this connection might lead or what the future might bring.

Around that time, my second oldest brother passed away. I was living abroad and unfortunately I could not attend his funeral or see him for the last time. That loss was very painful for me.

Only a few months later, another tragedy happened. My niece's father passed away.

I knew how much she loved her father, and I also knew how much her father loved her. He was everything to her. Losing him at such a young age was devastating. She was only about sixteen years old, maybe even a little younger.

Losing someone so close to us is one of the deepest pains we can experience in life. It is something we are never truly prepared for, and something we never expect to happen so suddenly. Her father was not an old man. He was still young, healthy, and strong. He could have lived another twenty or thirty years. But life does not always follow our expectations.

After his death, she was left feeling empty and lost. She still had her mother—who is one of my four sisters—and her two older brothers. She was the youngest in the family.

In the first few days after her father passed away, I called her to give my condolences. I didn't talk too much because I wanted to give her space and time to process her grief. She was still very young, and like many teenagers, she tried to stay strong and hide her feelings from others.

All of this happened before I traveled to visit my family. At that time I was still married, and my wife was visiting her own family. I was spending time with my two sons during the day. Like most children today, they were busy with school, friends, and social media, but we still tried to spend time together as father and sons.

Most nights, when it was daytime where my niece lived because of the time difference, we would talk. Our conversations continued regularly.

After her father passed away, she grew even closer to me. I could feel that she cared about me deeply as her uncle and respected me very much. A few times I tried to create some boundaries, because I didn't want her to become too emotionally dependent on me the way she had been with her father. I was afraid that one day she might feel the same pain again if I was no longer in her life.

But sometimes life takes its own path. Even now, as I write this book, she is still very close to me—just like my two sons.

Later in my life, as I became older, I sometimes wished I had a daughter. But that was no longer possible for me.

When my second son was born, my wife asked me if we should stop having more children. At the hospital, during the birth of our second son, she had a medical procedure so that she would not become pregnant again. My permission was required, and I agreed. At that time I still would have liked to have more children, but I respected her decision.

I was thirty-two years old when my second son was born. Even though we stopped having more children, I was grateful that I had two sons. Many people in this world hope to have even one child but cannot.

If you are reading this book, be grateful for what you have. Children are one of life's greatest blessings. Whether you have a son, a daughter, or both—remember that many people dream of having even one child.

Now it has been four years since my niece and I first got to know each other. During this time, our connection has grown very strong. Sometimes we can understand each other's feelings even without speaking—just by looking at each other.

In these four years we have laughed together, cried together, and shared many memories. If one day passes without us talking, it feels like a very long time for both of us. All of this happened naturally, without either of us realizing how deep our bond had become.

She cared about me so much that sometimes she even talked about living with me. I also liked the idea of having her around like my own daughter. But life is not always that simple. She has her mother to care for and her own future to focus on.

Because of that, we decided to leave things as they are and allow life to move forward naturally. If one day the right time comes, maybe it will happen. If not, that is also okay. We will continue living our lives and supporting each other from wherever we are.

It is very difficult for me to fully describe those four years, because every day was filled with emotions—hope, happiness, laughter, and sometimes tears. The relationship between my niece and me remains strong and continues to grow.

Neither of us ever imagined that someone could enter our lives after so many years and become so important.

Life is full of surprises—some painful and some beautiful. Always be ready for both.

The future is uncertain.

The past is full of lessons and sometimes pain.

But we still have one thing that truly belongs to us:

The present. Today.

Live it fully, and do not let it pass by and become only another painful memory of the past.

My niece eventually became like my two sons to me, especially after my divorce. During some periods of my life, when my sons were not always around me because of their own responsibilities—school for my younger son and work for my older son, the distance between us, and the fact that they were building their own lives—she was the person I spoke with the most.

Most of the time our conversations were online, through messages or sometimes video calls.

I never expected too much from my sons during that time. They had already gone through enough pain themselves growing up and seeing the difficulties in our family. I understood that they had their own lives, responsibilities, and struggles. I never expected them to visit me every day or constantly ask about my life. Instead, whenever I saw them, I tried to stay strong and not show them how much I was struggling inside.

I loved both of them deeply and always tried to treat them equally.

But my niece and I spent a lot of time talking, and through those conversations we began to understand each other more deeply.

She cared about me very much. Sometimes when the subject of death came up in our conversations and I mentioned that one day I would also leave this life, she became very upset and sad. I quickly realized that she did not like hearing me say such things.

Over time we became so used to each other that it almost felt like we were living our daily lives together, even though we were physically far apart. Our bodies were in different places, but in many ways our souls were connected.

When she heard that I wanted to participate in a singing competition, she became very happy. She constantly asked me about the date, the audition, and what songs I planned to sing. Whenever I sang for her, I was often critical of myself and felt that my voice was not good enough. But she always encouraged me and told me that my voice was special. I will explain more about my singing in the next chapter.

She was not the only person who said that, but her encouragement meant a lot to me.

She was not only someone who supported my dream of singing—she was also someone who was there for me during some of the hardest moments of my life. When I felt lonely, when I felt tired of life, or when everything seemed meaningless, she was someone I could talk to.

Without even realizing it, I became the same kind of support for her as well. If one day passed without us talking, she would feel sad and say that she missed me.

Unfortunately, life made it difficult for us to live closer to each other. I could not go and live with them for several reasons, including problems with the government in my country that I had already escaped from, as well as other complications. At the same time, she also had her own responsibilities and could not simply move to live with me.

Even so, our connection has remained strong.

Now, as I write these pages, I am still singing and doing my best to follow that path. I do not know what the future will bring, but I will continue to try. My connection with my niece is still strong today, and it is something that cannot easily be described in just a few pages.

Chapter 24

A Different Chapter of My Life

I slowly began getting used to my new life as a single person. But if I am honest, it was not easy at all. It may sound simple when you say it in words, but living it is something very different.

Even when you start adapting to a new life, the memories of the past never disappear. You still remember the good moments — the family life, the laughter, the feeling of belonging. Those memories stay with you, and sometimes they visit you when you least expect them.

After I lost my last investment — something I had been building for several years — I felt as if another piece of my life had collapsed. It was not only about the money. It was about the time, the hope, and the belief I had put into it.

After that loss, I left the shared accommodation where I had been living. The truth is, I did not know where to go or what to do next.

I applied for social housing, and they first placed me in a shared house where twelve people were living together, each person in a small room. There were strict rules. One of them was that if you came back after 10 p.m., you would not be allowed to enter the house and would have to spend the night outside.

After five days there, they moved me to another suburb, which was quite far from where my family lived. Because of the distance, I was not able to see my sons regularly. I also did not want them to come and see where I was living, because the place was not something I wanted them to see.

After those first five days, they transferred me again to a small flat in a building that had around forty similar units. Each flat had a small kitchen, a bathroom, and a place to sleep.

I cannot say it was bad, and I cannot say it was good. The reason is simple: many people in the world would be grateful to have a place like that to live in, while others would not be able to imagine spending even one hour there.

After three weeks of renting a temporary accommodation, I was told that if I wanted to stay longer, I would need to rent the flat at least for 3 months and then I can rent it again from them if they don't need it. Otherwise, I would have to leave. Since I had nowhere else to go, I decided to stay.

I paid the rent, the bills, and my living expenses, but time felt like it had stopped. Every day and every night inside that flat felt like a prison to me. I did not enjoy being there, but I had no other choice.

One day I planned to meet my younger son, but he was not able to come. Before going back to my flat, I went to the library. While I was there, I noticed a book that caught my attention. It was about Buddha.

I had already traveled to Thailand and noticed that many people there practiced Buddhism, either at home or by visiting temples, just like followers of other religions. I became curious and wanted to learn more, so I borrowed the book and started reading it.

What I discovered was very different from what I had expected. The book did not focus on religion in the traditional sense. Instead, it talked about human beings, about life, and about understanding ourselves. It felt more like a philosophy about humanity than a religion.

The ideas were interesting to me. The book described a group of Buddhist practitioners who followed a slightly different approach from other Buddhist communities. When I finished the book, my curiosity grew even more.

I searched online and eventually found the phone number and address of a local center connected to this practice. I called them and spoke with a lady who was very kind. I asked if I could visit the center to learn more. With my permission, she gave my contact details to another member.

A man called me a couple of days later, and we arranged to meet. When we met, he explained their beliefs to me — almost exactly the same things I had already read in the book. It was interesting because he did not know that I had already read about it.

Later, I visited their center during one of their monthly gatherings. People from different cultures attended — men and women from different backgrounds. Nothing was mandatory. You could come if you wanted, or not. Everything was voluntary.

I borrowed two more books from their small library. One of them was the autobiography of Tina Turner.

At that time, I did not even know who Tina Turner was. When I started reading the book, I discovered that she was a famous singer. But what impressed me was not her music — it was her life story.

She had gone through very difficult times, suffered greatly, and still found the strength to rebuild her life again.

Reading that book felt like a light turning on inside my mind.

It made me think: maybe I could also start again.

Even though I was no longer young, even though I was financially broken and emotionally exhausted, I told myself that I had nothing to lose by trying. If I tried and failed, at least I would know that I tried. But if I never tried at all, I would regret it for the rest of my life.

That thought stayed with me.

Even today, while writing this book, I am still trying to follow that idea. I continue moving forward, whether I succeed or not.

Looking back now, I realize that one of the most important things about my life is that I never stopped trying. Even when I lost, I tried again.

It was the same spirit that pushed me years earlier to move to another country in search of a better life — a place with more peace, stability, and opportunity. If I had given up back then, my life would have been very different. And also my two son's lives would be worse than mine.

From the beginning of this book, you may have already noticed that about me.

But please do not misunderstand me. I am not presenting myself as a knowledgeable person or someone who has all the answers. I am still learning, and I still make mistakes — just not the same mistakes I made before.

One thing I truly believe is this:

Anyone who refuses to accept their mistakes is only lying to themselves.

Deep inside, we all know when we make mistakes — just like we know the difference between right and left.

When I read the life story of Tina Turner and learned about her struggles in life and how she became famous later, it made me start thinking seriously about singing. Singing was something I had loved since I was a child.

Not only did I enjoy singing for myself, but I also sang for my niece after I started reconnecting with my sisters again. She was always very happy when I sang, and sometimes my songs even made her cry, because I was always a sad singer. For some reason, I was never able to sing happy songs.

Even when I was a child, I used to sing for my mother, and she loved my voice very much. When we were walking to school, I would sing for my friends, and they enjoyed listening. Deep inside, I always felt that my voice was good. But because of the life I lived and everything I went through, I never had the chance to even think about pursuing singing seriously.

Singing was something I loved, just like football, which I also enjoyed playing when I was young.

As I grew older, I started thinking more about life and the importance of wisdom, knowledge, and education. These things are very important in every person's life. As adults, we should teach younger generations what we have learned, including the mistakes we made, so they do not repeat them.

Many life lessons cannot be learned at school. Often, we only learn them after experiencing life ourselves. Sometimes we are lucky enough to learn by observing other people's lives or by having parents who teach us these lessons. But this is not always common.

One day I started asking myself: How can I become a singer?

I knew I was not very young anymore and that I was starting late, but I also believed that I would lose nothing if I tried.

So I began searching for a place to start. I searched online, made phone calls, sent emails, and asked people I knew. Unfortunately, I didn't get anywhere.

At that time I was living in a country where the main language was English, but my native language was different. I wanted to sing in my native language because singing in English required stronger grammar, better pronunciation, and more effort. I also had an accent, which made it even more difficult. Singing in my native language felt more natural to me. I could also sing in another language as well, so I had two languages I could use.

Sometimes I would even walk around on the streets hoping to hear someone speaking my language so I could ask them if they knew where I could start.

One day, after asking around, a woman who worked in a grocery shop gave me the names of a few Instagram accounts related to music and singing. She told me to follow them and send them messages asking if they could guide me in the right direction.

She also gave me the phone number of a woman who organized singers to perform in clubs and events. Unfortunately, that woman never answered my calls or replied to my message.

I followed the Instagram accounts and sent messages to them. One of them replied. I told him that I loved singing and that I was trying to find someone who could guide me to the right place.

He was a kind man. He told me to contact another person and said that this man might be able to help me.

I sent that man a message, and he asked me to record myself singing and send it to him. He said that after listening to it, he would let me know what he thought.

So I recorded two songs using only my voice and sent them to him. After listening, he told me that my voice was good but that I needed to learn more. He also suggested that it would be better if I could sing happy songs.

Later, I understood that the real issue was not my voice. The problem was that my singing style was sad. That was simply my natural tone and feeling. In music they call it timbre. Every singer has a different type of voice. Some voices fit happy songs, some sad songs, and some other styles.

I asked him if he knew someone who could teach singing so that I could improve my skills. He gave me a name and told me to search for it and contact that person.

I searched online, found the contact details, and called.

The man who answered the phone told me to come in so they could examine my voice and see whether I had potential.

I went there, and after a few tests he asked me to sing a song using only my voice. When I finished, he said that my voice was good and that I could join the classes if I wanted.

The classes cost money, and at that time it was difficult for me to afford it, but I still decided to register for one term.

At the beginning, he explained things in a way that sounded promising. But as time passed, I realized that I was not making much progress. Each week I had a half-hour lesson, and after each term he asked me to pay again.

Instead of helping me move forward, it felt like he was only practicing basic vocal exercises and delaying the real work. From the beginning he had told me that after two or three weeks we would go to a studio so I could try recording. But that never happened. Each week he would say, "next week" or "soon."

More than six months passed before I was finally able to record a song, and even then it was not easy. He wanted me to sing the way he preferred, not the way I naturally wanted to sing. I began to feel that he was trying to change my style into something that didn't feel like me.

During that same time, while I was living alone in that small flat far away from my sons, I was still searching for opportunities in my main language.

I remembered an old friend who was about 15 to 20 years older than me. I called him and asked if he knew anyone in the music industry or if there were any singing competitions I could join.

He told me he would ask around and get back to me.

One or two days later he sent me a phone number and a Facebook video link.

The phone number never replied.

But when I watched the Facebook video, I saw a woman who had finished third in a singing competition the previous year. In the video she said that if anyone believed they had a good voice and wanted to try, they should call the number she provided on her Facebook page.

I called the number from the Facebook page, and after some time they contacted me back. I asked if there was a singing competition and how I could join.

The lady on the phone told me that there was a competition coming up that year and that I could register if I wanted. The registration fee was not very expensive. She explained that I first needed to sing a song with only my voice and send it to them so they could listen and decide if my voice was suitable for the competition.

So I recorded a song and sent it to them. After that, I officially registered for the competition.

I asked her how the competition would work. She explained that the first audition would be only singing with no music at all — just our voice. Each contestant could choose their own song. At that stage there would be only the judges, the competitors, and the recording team, with no audience.

The second audition would also be a song we chose ourselves, but this time we could sing with music.

The final round would be performed in front of an audience.

There would be a two-week break between the first and second auditions, and then the final round would be about one month after the second audition.

After hearing this, I started practicing seriously. I told myself that this competition would be an experience for me. It did not matter whether I won or not. My goal was to gain experience. If I happened to win, that would be wonderful, but even if I didn't, I would still have learned something and finally done something I had dreamed about since I was a child.

At the same time, I was still attending singing lessons with the other coach in the second language I spoke. But after some time the lessons became frustrating. I had been attending once a week for around half an hour to forty-five minutes for almost six months, paying a lot of money, but I felt I was not making real progress.

He kept focusing on vocal exercises and repeatedly told me I was not ready yet to record properly. Each week he said, "Next week," or "You need more practice." Eventually, after almost six months, I finally recorded a song in his studio. But even then he continued saying that it was not good enough and that I needed more practice.

I began to feel that he was delaying the process while continuing to charge me for lessons that I did not really need anymore. I had already proven that I could sing.

During that same period, the competition in my main language had begun. I passed the first audition, then the second audition, and finally reached the final round.

The final included many talented singers — men and women of different ages. Some were very young, even the same age as my son. Others were middle-aged, and some were closer to my age.

For me, it was an amazing experience. Even though I did not win in the final round, that was not the most important thing for me. What mattered was that I gained experience, met new people, and for the first time in my life sang in front of an audience at the age of fifty.

One of the judges in the competition was a music producer, sound engineer, and musician who owned his own recording studio. Many years earlier he had worked with well-known singers.

After the competition ended, I started communicating with him.

One challenge I soon realized was that the country where I lived mainly spoke English, but my songs were in another language. Because of that, it was difficult for people in other countries who spoke my language to discover my music. I did not have many connections who could share my songs widely, so it was difficult for my voice to reach a larger audience.

After the competition finished, I contacted the judge who had the studio because I had been searching for someone who could help me record my songs properly.

He was a very kind and professional person. The good thing was that he spoke my language as well, even though he did not understand the second language I had recorded my first song in with the other coach.

During the competition he had already noticed that I had a good voice and the ability to sing, even though I had never formally studied music or singing before. I did not know how to play any musical instruments either, unlike many other singers who had studied music for years.

After some time, the first coach finally contacted me and said that my song was ready. He told me that the song and video had turned out very well after editing and mixing.

However, when I later asked the competition judge how much it usually cost to record a song, I discovered something shocking. The first coach had charged me almost five times more than the normal price, even though he had told me he was giving me a special discount.

When he finally sent me the finished song, I listened to it carefully. Unfortunately, I did not like it enough to share it publicly.

I asked him if I had the full rights to the song now that I had paid him completely. He confirmed that I did.

Even though I had already paid a deposit for three more songs, I decided not to continue working with him. It was not worth wasting more time and money.

Instead, I contacted the judge from the competition who owned the studio and explained everything that had happened.

I told him that I had already recorded a song but was not satisfied with the result. The only problem was that he did not understand the lyrics because they were in a language he did not speak. Still, I asked if he could listen to the song and give me his honest opinion, and if possible help me record it again.

He kindly agreed and asked me to send the song to him.

After listening to it, he called me back and said something that confirmed exactly what I had felt.

He said, "Your voice and emotions are good, and the video is good. But the music does not match your voice or the feeling of the song."

That was exactly what I had been thinking.

I asked him if there was any way to fix it.

He said yes. He suggested creating completely new music for the song and recording my voice again in his studio. He also offered to do the recording, mixing, and final production for a very small fee.

In fact, he said he would do most of the work as a gift because it was my first song.

He was a truly kind gentleman. He was not rich, but he had a generous heart and genuinely wanted to help people while still earning an honest living.

When I told him how much the first coach had charged me and how long I had waited just to record one song, he simply said:

"That's okay. Now you know how the industry works."

He also told me something that surprised me. After hearing me sing in the competition, he said I did not need a vocal coach anymore. I already knew how to sing naturally.

I sent him the video and audio from the first recording. He told me to give him a few days to create new music for the song.

A few days later he called me and invited me to his studio.

He had completely rearranged the music, added new elements, and improved the entire composition — even though he did not understand a single word of the lyrics.

If I say he was a professional, I truly mean it.

Before I even started thinking seriously about singing, I was in a very difficult place in my life. I was financially broken and emotionally exhausted. Reading the life story of Tina Turner opened something in my mind, but there was also another person who played an important role in encouraging me.

My niece was always motivating me to sing. She loved listening to my voice and the songs I sang. Many times when I was driving, I would record myself singing randomly and send the recording to her, or sometimes I would sing live for her. She always told me that my voice was special and that it sounded like it came from deep inside.

I only got to know her properly after she was already fifteen years old because, for many years, my sisters and I were not speaking to each other. Because of that, I had missed many moments with my family. When we finally reconnected, she became someone who always supported me.

Besides her, the only other person I told about my idea of becoming a singer was my younger son.

People sometimes ask how I started thinking about singing at that stage of my life.

The truth is that life itself pushed me toward that idea.

After the divorce, after all the financial losses, after spending so much time alone, I reached a point where I started thinking about myself for the first time in many years. For a long time my life has been about responsibility, family, work, and survival. Somewhere along the way, I had forgotten myself.

When I turned fifty, I knew that starting a singing career at that age was not early. But at the same time, I didn't think it was too late either. I also knew that success in music is never easy.

Still, I asked myself a simple question:

What do I have to lose if I try?

Singing was something I had always loved. It has been part of me since childhood. I told myself that even if I failed, at least I would be doing something I truly liked.

More importantly, I didn't want to reach an older age and look back with regret, asking myself why I never tried.

Of course, I sometimes wished I had started earlier — maybe when I was forty, thirty, or even in my twenties. But the reality is that my life circumstances were very different then. The path I walked brought me to this point much later.

Now I had something I didn't have before: time.

I had fewer responsibilities, and for the first time in many years I could focus a little on myself.

Becoming a professional football player at fifty would be almost impossible. Maybe becoming a singer at this age is also very difficult. But I decided to try anyway.

And even now, while I am writing this book, I am still trying.

After working with the sound producer I met through the competition, I re-recorded my first song with new music and shared it on social media. Not many people listened to it at first.

Later, I decided to record songs in the two languages I could sing in. I recorded one song in one language, then the next song in the other language, working in the studio with the sound engineer.

After my third song, I discussed the situation with the producer and some friends. They suggested that it might be better to focus on one language instead of two, at least for the beginning.

So I decided to concentrate on my main language.

By now, I have recorded four songs, and the fifth one will be released soon.

My songs are still not very popular. Not many people know about them yet, and that has been one of the biggest challenges. I tried to reach people in the music industry and asked them to listen to my voice and my songs, but it was very difficult to connect with anyone.

Sometimes it felt like every door was closed.

But I continued anyway.

Nothing in life comes easily. Everything takes time.

If I want to succeed, I must keep going. And if I don't succeed, at least I will know that I tried.

Trying and making mistakes is not losing.

The real loss happens when you stop trying and give up.

Mistakes teach us how to improve the next time. They teach patience and persistence.

And this lesson is not only about music.
It is about life itself.

Before finishing this book, however, I want to share two very important experiences from my life.

The next two chapters will talk about the deepest pain I went through and the lessons that came from those experiences. These are real events from my life. They are not stories created for a book.

Every word I have written here comes from the life I lived, the struggles I faced, and the emotions I felt.

They come from my heart to yours.

Chapter 25

The Deepest Pain

Opening

Pain is something every human being experiences in life. No one escapes it. It comes in different forms and at different moments in our lives. Sometimes it comes quietly, and sometimes it arrives like a storm that changes everything.

Throughout my life I experienced many different types of pain. Some of them were easier to overcome, and others stayed with me for years. When you go through difficult moments, you slowly begin to understand that pain is also a teacher. It shows you parts of life you never understood before.

Looking back now, I can see that my life was shaped by many painful experiences. Each one left a mark on me, but each one also taught me something.

Some pains come from losing people we love.

Some pains come from broken relationships.

Others come from losing the things we worked so hard to build.

And sometimes the deepest pain comes from something even harder to explain.

The Pain of Losing People

One of the most difficult pains in life is losing someone you love. When a person you care about disappears from your life forever, it leaves a space that can never truly be filled again.

I experienced this pain when my brother passed away. At that time I was living abroad and I was not able to attend his funeral or say goodbye to him for the last time. That feeling stayed with me for a long time.

Losing someone without having the chance to see them one last time is something that stays in your heart. You keep thinking about the moments you shared together and the things you never had the chance to say.

Later in my life, about a year and a half ago, I also lost both of my parents. Once again I was not able to be there to see them for the last time or attend their funerals. This was another very deep pain for me.

Even though I was already in my fifties, when I lost my mother I felt like I had lost one of the most valuable things in my life.

Close family members are not replaceable. A mother and father come only once in our lives. We often do not realize their true value until the day they are gone forever.

The same is true for brothers and sisters.

In my opinion, children are also one of the greatest blessings in life. After that came our nephews and nieces. A husband or wife is also important, but there is something different about family.

Why do I say that?

Because if we lose our mother or father, we can never replace them. The same is true for brothers and sisters. When they leave this life, no one can take their place.

I had six brothers. When my second brother passed away, none of my other brothers could replace him. Each person is unique, and each relationship is special in its own way.

Partners in life are also important, but it is possible during a lifetime to meet another partner and build a new relationship. With parents and siblings, that is not possible.

My mother was very old, but every day she asked about me. Even though I had two sons of my own, she still worried about me like I was a child.

She asked if I had eaten.

She asked how my health was.

She asked if everything in my life was okay.

She loved her children more than herself.

After she passed away, I realized that there was no one else in the world who would ask about me the same way my mother did.

That was the moment I truly understood what I had lost.

Sometimes we also carry regret. We think about the things we wanted to do for our parents when we were younger but never had the chance to do.

If your mother is still alive, do everything you can to make her happy.

Do the same for your father.

And do not forget your brothers and sisters if you have them. Family is one of the greatest gifts life gives us.

The Pain of Broken Relationships

Another kind of pain that many people experience in life is the pain of broken relationships.

After many years of marriage, I went through a divorce that changed my life completely. When you spend many years building a life with someone, raising children together, and sharing responsibilities, you never imagine that one day everything might fall apart.

But sometimes life takes directions we never expected.

When a relationship breaks after many years, it is not only the relationship that ends. It can feel like a part of your identity disappears as well.

You ask yourself many questions.

You think about the past.

You remember the good moments and the difficult ones.

And slowly you try to accept that life has changed.

The Pain of Losing What You Built

Another difficult experience I went through was losing the investments and financial stability that I had worked for over many years.

Building something takes time, patience, and effort. When you lose it, it can feel like years of your life disappeared in a moment.

Financial loss is not only about money. It also affects your confidence and your sense of security. It makes you question your decisions and your future.

But even though money can be lost, life continues.

The Pain of Loneliness

After the divorce and the many changes in my life, I also experienced a deep sense of loneliness.

For many years I had lived with my family, surrounded by people and responsibilities. Suddenly life became quiet.

My sons had their own lives to focus on—school, work, and their own future. I understood that this was natural, and I never wanted them to feel responsible for my happiness.

But there were many moments when I felt alone.

Loneliness is not always about being physically alone. Sometimes it is about feeling that no one truly understands what you are going through.

The Deepest Pain

But after experiencing all of these things, I realized something important.

The deepest pain in life is not losing money.

It is not even divorce. And it is not only the loss of people we love.

The deepest pain is when someone breaks your heart in a way you never imagined.

When the person you trusted, the person you loved, the person you believed would always stand beside you, becomes the one who hurts you the most.

It is the pain that comes when someone you felt very close to lets you down in a way you never expected.

When that happens, the heart can break so deeply that it changes how you feel about everything.

After experiencing that kind of pain, many things in life begin to feel different.

The things that once made you happy may not feel the same anymore.

The things that once upset you may no longer affect you the same way.

It can feel like something inside you has become quiet.

There were moments in my life when I felt that life itself had lost its meaning. Moments when the future felt empty and uncertain.

But even during those difficult times, something inside me continued to search for a reason to keep moving forward.

For me, one of those reasons became music.

Singing became a way for me to express emotions that were difficult to explain with words. It gave me something to focus on and something to hope for.

At the same time, the people who remained close to me—my sons and my niece—reminded me that life still had meaning.

Pain may change us, but it does not have to destroy us.

Sometimes the deepest pain can also become the beginning of a new chapter in our lives.

Chapter 26

The Lessons Life Taught Me

After experiencing deep pain and rediscovering myself through music, I began to understand the lessons life had quietly been teaching me all along.

Life is a long journey filled with many experiences. Some bring happiness, and others bring pain. As we move through life, we slowly begin to understand that every experience—good or bad—teaches us something.

When I look back at my life, I realize that many of the most important lessons I learned did not come from the easy moments. They came from the difficult times, the losses, and the struggles.

Pain has a strange way of teaching us things that comfort never could.

Over the years life taught me many lessons. Some of them became very clear to me only after many years had passed.

Family Is One of the Most Important Things in Life

One of the greatest lessons life taught me is the importance of family.

When you grow up and begin to understand yourself, your life, and the world around you, do not rush to blame your parents for their mistakes, their lifestyle, or their choices.

You were not there when they were young.

You do not know the difficulties they faced.

You do not know the sacrifices they made so you could grow up.

Remember that they were also experiencing life for the first time, just like you are now.

If your parents are still alive, be grateful for them. If they have passed away, remember them with respect and understanding.

Family members may not be perfect, but they are part of the roots that helped shape who we become.

Ask Questions and Keep Learning

When you are young, especially during your teenage years, it is normal to feel lost and unsure about the future.

At that stage of life, do not be afraid to ask questions.

Learn from people who already have experience in life. This could be your parents, relatives, friends, teachers, or even people you do not personally know but who have achieved something meaningful.

Do not be shy to ask for advice.

No one knows everything in life, and the person who thinks they know everything usually understands very little.

When you ask questions, you learn faster.

But at the same time, be careful not to believe everything you hear. Listen to different perspectives and think for yourself.

Wisdom often comes from listening, observing, and learning from many sources.

Understand Life Before Making Big Decisions

Some of the most important decisions in life require preparation and understanding.

Marriage is one of them.

Many people think of marriage only as love, attraction, or companionship. But marriage is much more than that. It is a partnership that requires patience, respect, responsibility, and understanding.

Before getting married, people should try to understand what marriage truly means.

How do you treat your partner?

How do you solve problems together?

How do you deal with disagreements and difficulties?

These are important questions.

If you are a parent, teach your children about these things. Let them understand that marriage is not only about emotions or physical attraction. It is about building a life together.

And above everything else, learn how to treat each other as human beings with respect and dignity.

Create Your Own Path

Another lesson life taught me is that we should not wait for miracles to change our lives.

Many people wait for something magical to happen that will suddenly improve their lives.

But the truth is that the only person who can truly change your life is you.

The real miracle happens when you wake up in the morning and take action. It happens when you work hard, struggle, make mistakes, learn from them, and continue moving forward.

Success rarely happens overnight.

It requires patience, effort, and persistence.

Life does not reward us simply because we are good people. Life rewards effort, discipline, and the work we put into our goals.

Forgiveness

Another important lesson is the power of forgiveness.

In life, people will sometimes hurt you. Friends, relatives, and even people you love may make mistakes.

When that happens, try to forgive them.

Friends may come and go throughout life, but family often remains part of our lives forever.

Sometimes conflicts happen because both sides see things differently. Instead of only believing that we are right, we should also try to understand the perspective of others.

Forgiveness does not mean forgetting everything that happened. It means choosing peace instead of carrying anger for the rest of your life.

One day we may lose the chance to repair a relationship forever. When someone passes away, we can no longer fix what was broken.

That is when regret begins.

Do not wait for that moment.

If you can forgive someone today, do it.

And just as importantly, learn to forgive yourself for the mistakes you made in the past.

Love Without Conditions

Love should not always come with conditions.

If you love your parents, love them because they are your parents, not only because of what they have done for you.

The same is true with children.

Parents should guide their children but not pressure them too much. Every person needs time to grow, make mistakes, and learn from them.

We were all young once. We also made mistakes.

Do not constantly compare your children with others.

And as children, do not compare your parents with other parents.

Every family is different, and every life path is unique.

Follow Your Dreams

Another lesson life taught me is to follow your dreams.

Many people stop trying after the first failure. Others believe they are too old, not talented enough, or that it is already too late.

But every successful person started somewhere.

The difference is that they did not give up.

If you truly want to achieve something, you must keep trying even when things do not work the first time.

Dreams alone are not enough.

Dreams without action remain only dreams.

When you take action, work hard, fail, try again, and continue moving forward, you slowly move closer to your goal.

Take Responsibility for Your Life

It is easy to blame others when things go wrong in our lives.

But a simple reminder can help us see things differently.

Look at your hand.

You have five fingers. When you point your index finger at someone else to blame them, the other four fingers are pointing back at you.

Before blaming others, always ask yourself what you could have done differently.

Personal responsibility is one of the most powerful tools for growth.

Do Not Let Fear of Death Stop You From Living

Death is a reality that every human being will face one day.

But thinking constantly about death should not stop us from living.

Life is short. Sometimes it passes faster than we expect.

During my life I experienced dangerous situations. I lived through war, crossed the ocean, and faced moments where death felt very close.

But fear cannot become the reason we stop living.

If you spend your life afraid and doing nothing, it is almost like you are slowly killing your own spirit before your real time comes.

Stand up. Fight for your life. Try to enjoy it while you are still alive.

Life Continues to Teach Us

Even now, life continues to teach me new lessons.

Every stage of life brings new challenges and new understanding.

The important thing is to remain open to learning.

Sometimes the lessons come through happiness, and sometimes they come through pain.

But if we pay attention, every experience can help us grow.

My journey is still continuing, and I am still learning.

Final Message to the Reader

If you have read this book until this page, I want to thank you from the bottom of my heart.

Everything you read in these pages came from real life. These are not stories created by imagination. They are experiences, pain, lessons, and moments that shaped the person I became today.

Life is not always easy. Sometimes it gives us happiness, sometimes it gives us pain. Sometimes we lose the people we love. Sometimes we lose the life we built and we are forced to start again from the beginning.

But no matter how difficult life becomes, we must remember one important thing: we should never give up.

Pain can break us, but it can also teach us. It can make us stronger, wiser, and more understanding of others. Every challenge in life carries a lesson inside it.

If there is one thing I learned from my journey, it is this:

Life is not about how many times you fall. It is about how many times you stand up again.

I also want to say something to my sons.

My dear sons, if one day you read this book and understand more about my life and my journey, remember that you were always the most important part of my life.

No matter what happened in our lives, and no matter where life takes us in the future, my love for you will never change.

You were, and you will always be, in my heart.

And to the younger generation who may read this book one day, I want to tell you something simple: follow your dreams, respect others, love your family, forgive when you can, and never allow difficulties to stop you from living your life.

Your life is a journey, and every step — even the painful ones — can lead you toward purpose.

If my story helps even one person feel stronger, or gives someone hope during a difficult moment, then writing this book was worth it.

Thank you for being part of my journey.

— Sami Walker

"In the end, it is not the world outside that defines us, but the heart and soul we carry inside."

Thank you for reading *From Pain to Purpose*.

If this story touched you or gave you hope, please consider leaving a short review on Amazon. Your words help other readers discover this book and support independent authors like me.

With gratitude,

SAMI WALKER